How to Be an Even Better Manager

Tenth edition

How to Be an Even Better Manager

A complete A–Z of proven
techniques and essential skills

Michael Armstrong

KoganPage

First published in Great Britain in 1983, entitled *How to Be a Better Manager*
Second edition, 1988, entitled *How to Be an Even Better Manager*
Tenth edition 2017

2nd Floor, 45 Gee Street	c/o Martin P Hill Consulting	4737/23 Ansari Road
London	122 W 27th St, 10th Floor	Daryaganj
EC1V 3RS	New York, NY 10001	New Delhi 110002
United Kingdom	USA	India

www.koganpage.com

© Michael Armstrong, 1983, 1988, 1990, 1994, 1999, 2004, 2008, 2011, 2014, 2017

The right of Michael Armstrong to be identified as the author of this work has been asserted by him in accordance with the Copyright, Designs and Patents Act 1988.

ISBN   978 0 7494 8027 1
E-ISBN   978 0 7494 8028 8

British Library Cataloguing-in-Publication Data

A CIP record for this book is available from the British Library.

Library of Congress Cataloging-in-Publication Data

Names: Armstrong, Michael, 1928- author.
Title: How to be an even better manager : a complete a-z of proven techniques and essential skills / Michael Armstrong.
Description: Tenth edition. | New York, NY : Kogan Page Ltd, [2017] | Revised edition of the author's How to be an even better manager, 2014. | Includes index.
Identifiers: LCCN 2017014451 (print) | LCCN 2017013829 (ebook) | ISBN 9780749480288 (ebook) | ISBN 9780749480271 (pbk.)
Subjects: LCSH: Management.
Classification: LCC HD31 (print) | LCC HD31 .A73 2017 (ebook) | DDC 658.4–dc23
LC record available at https://lccn.loc.gov/2017013829

Typeset by Integra Software Services, Pondicherry
Print production managed by Jellyfish
Printed and bound by CPI Group (UK) Ltd, Croydon CR0 4YY

CONTENTS

PREFACE TO THE TENTH EDITION

This tenth edition of *How to Be an Even Better Manager* covers 56 key aspects of management and has been extensively revised since the ninth edition was published in 2014. Four new chapters have been added and others have been extensively revised.

The book therefore covers a wide range of the skills and approaches used by effective managers – what they need to understand and be able to do to be fully competent in their roles.

It will be an invaluable handbook for existing and aspiring managers, and will be particularly useful for those seeking to obtain qualifications in management or those studying for the Leading, Managing and Developing People and Developing Skills for Business Leadership modules of the Chartered Institute of Personnel and Development qualification scheme.

HOW TO USE THIS BOOK

This book is for those who want to develop their managerial skills and competences. It covers all the key skills that managers use, and refers to the main aspects of managing people, activities and themselves with which they need to be familiar.

You can dip into this book at any point – each chapter is self-contained – but it would be useful to read Chapter 1 first. This defines the overall concept of management and the areas in which managers need to be competent, thus providing a framework for the succeeding chapters, which deal with the specific skills and techniques involved in managing people and processes.

How to be a   01
better manager

Better managers recognize that the art of management is something
they need to learn. No one becomes a fully competent manager
overnight. There are, of course, many ways of learning how to be
an effective manager. There is no doubt that experience is the best
teacher – the time you have spent as a manager or team leader and
your analysis of how good managers you come across operate. You
can learn from your own boss and from other bosses. This means
accepting what you recognize as effective behaviour and rejecting
what is inappropriate – that is, behaviour that fails to provide the
leadership and motivation required from good managers and that
does not deliver results.

There is an old saying: 'People learn to manage by managing
under the guidance of a good manager.' This is just as true today,
but to make the best use of experience it is helpful to place it in a
framework that defines your understanding of what management is
about, and helps you to reflect on and analyse your own experience
and the behaviour of others. There is also a wealth of knowledge
about the skills that managers need to use and the aspects of managing people, activities and themselves that they need to understand.
None of these skills provides a quick fix that is universally applicable. It is useful to know about them, but it is also necessary to
develop an understanding of how they are best applied and modified to meet the particular demands of the situation in which you
find yourself. This is not a prescriptive book – 'Do this and all will
be well' – rather, its aim is to present approaches that have been
proved to be generally effective.

But they have to be adapted to suit your own style of managing and the circumstances where their application is required.

To become a better manager, it is necessary to develop each of the 50 areas of skills and knowledge covered by this handbook.

But you will be better prepared to do this if you have a general understanding of the process of management. This will provide a framework into which you can fit the various approaches and techniques described in each chapter. The aim of this introductory chapter is to provide such a framework under the following headings:

- what management is about;
- the aims of management;
- the purpose of management and leadership;
- the processes of management;
- managerial roles;
- the distinction between management and leadership;
- the fragmentary nature of managerial work;
- what managers actually do;
- what managers can do about it;
- managerial qualities;
- managerial effectiveness;
- developing managerial effectiveness.

What management is about

Essentially, management is about deciding what to do and then getting it done through people. This definition emphasizes that people are the most important resource available to managers. It is through this resource that all other resources – processes and systems knowledge, finance, materials, plant, equipment, etc – will be managed.

However, managers are there to achieve results. To do this they have to deal with events and eventualities. They may do this primarily through people, but an overemphasis on the people content of management diverts attention from the fact that in managing events, managers must be personally involved. They manage themselves as well as other people. They cannot delegate everything. They frequently have to rely on their own resources to get things done. These resources consist of experience, know-how, skill, competences and time, all of which must be deployed not only in directing and motivating people, but also in understanding situations and issues, problem analysis and definition, decision-making and taking direct action themselves as well as through other people. They will get support, advice and assistance from their staff, but in the last analysis they are on their own. They have to make the decisions and they have to initiate and sometimes take the action. A chairman fighting a takeover bid will get lots of advice, but he or she will personally manage the crisis, talking directly to the financial institutions, merchant banks, financial analysts, City editors and the mass of shareholders.

The basic definition of management should therefore be extended to read, 'deciding what to do and then getting it done through the effective use of resources'. The most important part of management will indeed be getting things done through people, but managers will be concerned directly or indirectly with all other resources, including their own.

The aims of management

Management is a process that exists to get results by making the best use of the human, financial and material resources available to the organization and to individual managers. It is very much concerned with adding value by the use of these resources, and this added value depends on the expertise and commitment of the people who are responsible for managing the business.

The purpose of management and leadership

The Management Standards Centre stated that the key purpose of management and leadership is to 'provide direction, facilitate change and achieve results through the efficient, creative and responsible use of resources'. These purposes were analysed as follows.

Providing direction

- Develop a vision for the future.
- Gain commitment and provide leadership.
- Provide governance – comply with values, ethical and legal frameworks and manage risks in line with shared goals.

Facilitating change

- Lead innovations.
- Manage change.

Achieving results

- Lead the business to achieve goals and objectives.
- Lead operations to achieve specific results.
- Lead projects to achieve specified results.

Meeting customer needs

- Promote products and/or services to customers.
- Obtain contracts to supply products and/or services.
- Deliver products and/or services to customers.
- Solve problems for customers.
- Assure the quality of products and/or services.

Working with people

- Build relationships.
- Develop networks and partnerships.
- Manage people.

Using resources

- Manage financial resources.
- Procure products and/or services.
- Manage physical resources and technology.
- Manage information and knowledge.

Managing self and personal skills

- Manage own contribution.
- Develop own knowledge, skills and competence.

The processes of management

The overall process of management is subdivided into a number of individual processes that are methods of operation specially designed to assist in the achievement of objectives. Their purpose is to bring as much system, order, predictability, logic and consistency to the task of management as possible in the ever-changing, varied and turbulent environment in which managers work. The main processes of management were defined by the classical theorists of management as:

- Planning – deciding on a course of action to achieve a desired result.
- Organizing – setting up and staffing the most appropriate organization to achieve the aim.

- Motivating – exercising leadership to motivate people to work together smoothly and to the best of their ability as part of a team.

- Controlling – measuring and monitoring the progress of work in relation to the plan and taking corrective action when required.

But this classical view has been challenged by the empiricists, such as Rosemary Stewart[1] and Henry Mintzberg,[2] who studied how managers actually spend their time. They observed that the work of managers is fragmented, varied and subject to continual adjustment. It is governed to a large degree by events over which managers have little control and by a dynamic network of interrelationships with other people.

Managers attempt to control their environment but sometimes it controls them. They may consciously or unconsciously seek to plan, organize, direct and control, but their days almost inevitably become a jumbled sequence of events.

To the empiricists, management is a process involving a mix of rational, logical, problem-solving and decision-making activities, and intuitive, judgemental activities. It is therefore both science and art.

Managers carry out their work on a day-to-day basis in conditions of variety, turbulence and unpredictability. A single word to describe all these features would be chaos. Tom Peters,[3] however, has suggested that it is possible for managers to thrive on chaos.

Managers also have to be specialists in ambiguity, with the ability to cope with conflicting and unclear requirements, as Rosabeth Moss Kanter[4] has demonstrated.

Managerial roles

During the course of a typical day, a chief executive may well meet the marketing director to discuss the programme for launching a new product, the HR director to decide how best to reorganize the distribution department, the production director to ask why costs per unit of output are going up and what he or she is going to do about it, and the finance director to review the latest set of management accounts before the next board meeting.

He or she may have had to meet a journalist to be interviewed about how the company is going to deliver better results next year. Lunch may have been taken with a major customer, and the evening spent at a business dinner. Some of these activities could be categorized under the headings of planning, organizing, directing and controlling, but chief executives would not have attached these labels when deciding how to spend their time (in so far as there was any choice). The fact that these processes took place was imposed by the situation and the need to take on one or more of the roles inherent in the manager's job. These roles are fundamentally concerned with:

- getting things done – planning ahead, maintaining momentum and making things happen;
- finding out what is going on;
- reacting to new situations and problems;
- responding to demands and requests.

They involve a great deal of interpersonal relations, communicating, information processing and decision-making.

The distinction between management and leadership

Managers have to be leaders and leaders are often, but not always, managers. But a distinction can be made between the processes of management and leadership.

Management is concerned with achieving results by effectively obtaining, deploying, utilizing and controlling all the resources required, namely people, money, information, facilities, plant and equipment.

Leadership focuses on the most important resource, people. It is the process of developing and communicating a vision for the future, motivating people and gaining their commitment and engagement.

The distinction is important. Management is mainly about the provision, deployment, utilization and control of resources. But where people are involved – and they almost always are – it is impossible to deliver results without providing effective leadership. It is not enough to be a good manager of resources, you also have to be a good leader of people.

The fragmentary nature of managerial work

Because of the open-ended nature of their work, managers feel compelled to perform a great variety of tasks at an unrelenting pace. Research into how managers spend their time confirms that their activities are characterized by fragmentation, brevity and variety. This arises for the following six reasons:

1 Managers are largely concerned with dealing with people – their staff and their internal and external customers. But people's behaviour is often unpredictable; their demands and responses are conditioned by the constantly changing circumstances in which they exist, the pressures to which they have to respond and their individual wants and needs. Conflicts arise and have to be dealt with on the spot.

2 Managers are not always in a position to control the events that affect their work. Sudden demands are imposed upon them from other people within the organization or from outside. Crises can occur that they are unable to predict.

3 Managers are expected to be decisive and deal with situations as they arise. Their best-laid plans are therefore often disrupted; their established priorities have to be abandoned.

4 Managers are subject to the beck and call of their superiors, who also have to respond instantly to new demands and crises.

5 Managers often work in conditions of turbulence and ambiguity. They are not clear about what is expected of them when new situations arise. They therefore tend to be reactive rather than proactive, dealing with immediate problems rather than trying to anticipate them.

6 For all the reasons given above, managers are subject to constant interruptions. They have little chance to settle down and think about their plans and priorities or to spend enough time in studying control information to assist in maintaining a 'steady state' as far as their own activities go.

What managers actually do

What managers do will be dependent on their function, level, organization (type, structure, culture, size) and their working environment generally (the extent to which it is turbulent, predictable, settled, pressurized, steady). Individual managers will adapt to these circumstances in different ways and will operate more or less successfully in accordance with their own perceptions of the behaviour expected of them, their experience of what has or has not worked in the past, and their own personal characteristics.

There are, however, the following typical characteristics of managerial work.

Reaction and non-reflection

Much of what managers do is, of necessity, an unreflecting response to circumstances. Managers are usually not so much slow and methodical decision-makers as doers who have to react rapidly to problems as they arise and think on their feet. Much time is spent in day-to-day troubleshooting.

Choice

Managers can often exercise choice about their work. They informally negotiate widely different interpretations of the boundaries and dimensions of ostensibly identical jobs, with particular emphasis upon the development of 'personal domain' (ie establishing their own territory and the rules that apply within it).

Communication

Much managerial activity consists of asking or persuading others to do things, which involves managers in face-to-face verbal communication of limited duration. Communication is not simply what managers spend a great deal of time doing but the medium through which managerial work is constituted.

Identification of tasks

The typical work of a junior manager is the 'organizational work' of drawing upon an evolving stock of knowledge about 'normal' procedures and routines in order to identify and negotiate the accomplishment of problems and tasks.

Character of the work

The character of work varies by duration, time span, recurrence, unexpectedness and source. Little time is spent on any one activity or, in particular, on the conscious, systematic formulation of plans. Planning and decision-making tend to take place in the course of other activities. Managerial activities are riven by contradictions, cross-pressures, and the need to cope with and reconcile conflict. Managers spend a lot of time accounting for and explaining what they do, in informal relationships and in 'participating'.

What managers can do about it

To a degree, managers have simply to put up with the circumstances in which they work as described above – they have to manage in conditions of turbulence, uncertainty and ambiguity. That is why one of the characteristics of effective managers is their resilience – they have to be able to cope with these inevitable pressures. But there are competencies as described below and skills as discussed in the rest of this book that can help them to manage in these circumstances. To a considerable extent, it is up to managers to be aware of these requirements, the behaviours expected of them and the skills they can use to help in carrying out their often-demanding responsibilities. They must treat these as guidelines for personal development plans.

Managers can learn from the example of their bosses, by guidance from those bosses and from mentors, and through formal training courses, but self-managed learning is all-important. The starting point is an understanding of the key managerial qualities and the criteria for measuring managerial effectiveness, as described in the next two sections.

Managerial qualities

Michael Pedler and his colleagues[5] suggested on the basis of their extensive research that there are 11 qualities or attributes that are possessed by successful managers:

- command of basic facts;
- relevant professional knowledge;
- continuing sensitivity to events;
- analytical, problem-solving and decision/judgement-making skills;
- social skills and abilities;
- emotional resilience;
- proactivity;
- creativity;
- mental agility;
- balanced learning habits and skills;
- self-knowledge.

Studies carried out on the qualities displayed by successful top managers as quoted by Rosemary Stewart[1] show a number of common characteristics, such as:

- willingness to work hard;
- perseverance and determination;
- willingness to take risks;
- ability to inspire enthusiasm;
- toughness.

Managerial effectiveness

As a manager and a leader you will be judged not only on the results you have achieved but on the level of competence you have attained and applied in getting those results. Competence is about knowledge and skills – what people need to know and be able to do to carry out their work well.

You will also be judged on how you do your work – how you behave in using your knowledge and skills. These are often defined as 'behavioural competencies' and can be defined as those aspects of management behaviour that lead to effective performance. They refer to the personal characteristics that people bring to their work roles in such areas as leadership, teamworking, flexibility and communication.

Many organizations have developed competency frameworks that define what they believe to be the key competencies required for success. Such frameworks are used to inform decisions on selection, management development and promotion.

Importantly, they can provide the headings under which the performance of managers and other staff is assessed. Managers who want to get on need to know what the framework is, and the types of behaviour expected of them in each of the areas it covers.

The following is an example of a competency framework:

- *Achievement/results orientation*. The desire to get things done well and the ability to set and meet challenging goals, create own measures of excellence and constantly seek ways of improving performance.

- *Business awareness*. The capacity to continually identify and explore business opportunities, understand the business opportunities and priorities of the organization and constantly seek methods of ensuring that the organization becomes more businesslike.

- *Communication*. The ability to communicate clearly and persuasively, orally or in writing.

- *Customer focus*. The exercise of unceasing care in looking after the interests of external and internal customers to ensure that their wants, needs and expectations are met or exceeded.

- *Developing others*. The desire and capacity to foster the development of members of their team, providing feedback, support, encouragement and coaching.

- *Flexibility*. The ability to adapt to and work effectively in different situations and to carry out a variety of tasks.

- *Leadership*. The capacity to inspire individuals to give of their best to achieve a desired result and to maintain effective relationships with individuals and the team as a whole.

- *Planning*. The ability to decide on courses of action, ensuring that the resources required to implement the action will be available and scheduling the programme of work required to achieve a defined end result.

- *Problem-solving*. The capacity to analyse situations, diagnose problems, identify the key issues, establish and evaluate alternative courses of action, and produce a logical, practical and acceptable solution.

- *Teamwork*. The ability to work cooperatively and flexibly with other members of the team, with a full understanding of the role to be played as a team member.

Some organizations illustrate their competency frameworks with examples of positive or negative indicators of performance under each heading. These provide a useful checklist for managers willing to measure their own performance in order to develop their career.

Developing managerial effectiveness

The development of managerial effectiveness should be focused on the qualities and competencies listed above. The fundamental question that is addressed by this book is: 'How can I learn to be a manager?'

A familiar answer to this question is to say that 'managers learn from experience'. But can experience alone be the best teacher? Several writers have expressed their doubts on this score. Tennyson called it a 'dirty nurse'. Oscar Wilde noted that 'experience is the name everyone gives to their mistakes'. And the historian Froude wrote that 'experience teaches slowly and at the cost of mistakes'.

Experience is an essential way of learning to improve but it is an imperfect instrument. We also need guidance from a good manager and from other sources such as this book that will help us to interpret our experience, learn from our mistakes and make better use of our experience in the future.

What you can do

Perhaps Francis Bacon provided the best answer to this question when he wrote: 'Studies perfect nature and are perfected by experience.' The art of management, and it is an art, is important enough to be studied. The aim of such studies should be to help us to make better use of our natural attributes – our personality and intelligence – and to ensure that past experience is better interpreted and more fully used, and that future experience is more quickly and purposefully absorbed. The rest of this book provides practical guidance on what you need to know and be able to do in order to become a better manager.

10 fundamental ways of becoming a better manager

1 Know where you are, where you are going, how you are going to get there and how you will know you have arrived.

2 Aim to master the present and pre-empt the future.

3 Communicate effectively – about what is happening, why it is happening, what is going to happen and why.

4 Make it clear to people what you expect them to do.

5 Realize each person is different.

6 Let people know how they are getting on.

7 Let people make mistakes.

8 Be prepared to say 'no'.

9 Don't worry about being liked.

10 Build trust.

Endnotes

1 Stewart, R (1967) *Managers and Their Jobs*, Macmillan, London

2 Mintzberg, H (1987) Crafting strategy, *Harvard Business Review*, July–August

3 Peters, T (1988) *Thriving on Chaos*, Macmillan, London

4 Kanter, R M (1989) *When Giants Learn to Dance*, Simon & Schuster, London

5 Pedler, M, Burgoyne, J and Boydell, T (1986) *A Manager's Guide to Self-Development*, McGraw-Hill, Maidenhead

PART ONE
Managing people

How to treat people right   02

Treating people right means treating them fairly and with respect. But it is not about going soft on them. It is necessary to be firm as well as fair, to set standards and to ensure that they are met. Ed Lawler,[1] a leading American management expert, wrote that 'treating people right is a fundamental key to creating organizational effectiveness'. He also noted that the concept of treating people right recognizes the fact that 'both organizations and individuals need to succeed. One cannot succeed without the other'.

The seven principles of treating people right are:

1 Treat people with respect.
2 Treat people fairly.
3 Create the right work environment.
4 Help people to develop their capabilities and skills.
5 Provide leadership.
6 Get to know team members.
7 Define expectations and ensure they are met.

Treat people with respect

To respect someone is to recognize a person's qualities, ensuring that they feel valued and treating them with dignity and courtesy – no belittling, no bullying. It means being sensitive to the differences between people, taking this diversity into account in any dealings with them. It involves honouring their contribution and listening to what they have to say. It also means recognizing that people may have legitimate grievances and responding to them promptly, fully and sympathetically.

Treat people fairly

Treating people fairly means that you should:

- give proper consideration to their views and circumstances;
- apply policies and decisions consistently to all concerned;
- provide adequate explanations of decisions made (transparency);
- avoid personal bias with regard to individuals or categories of people (no favouritism);
- ensure that people are rewarded equitably in comparison with others in the organization in accordance with their contribution;
- see that people get what was promised to them (deliver the deal);
- define the standards people are expected to achieve;
- indicate clearly to people where you believe that the defined standards are not being reached and give them a chance to improve.

Create the right work environment

People should feel that their work is worthwhile. Their jobs should make good use of their skills and abilities and as far as possible provide some autonomy so that they have a reasonable degree of control over their activities and decisions. Employees also need feedback – information about how well they are doing, preferably obtained for themselves from their work rather than from their manager. As described in Chapter 3, these are all factors that, if they are present in jobs, will increase intrinsic motivation – motivation from the work itself. They can be considerably influenced by the ways in which work is organized – the design of the work system.

The fundamental requirement is for the work system to operate efficiently and flexibly. It is necessary to provide for the smooth flow of processes and activities and ensure that resources – people, materials, plant, equipment and money – are used effectively. But in designing or managing a work system it is also necessary to consider what needs to be done to treat people right. The system should enable employees to gain fulfilment from their work by as far as possible allowing scope for variety, challenge and autonomy. It should provide a good environment in terms of working conditions and a healthy and safe system of work, bearing in mind the need to minimize stress and pay attention to ergonomic considerations in the design of equipment and work stations.

Help people to develop their capabilities and skills

It is in your own interest and that of your organization to enhance the skills and capabilities of the people you manage through coaching, training and, importantly, giving them scope to learn or develop skills by providing new work opportunities or challenges. In doing so you will be 'treating them right'. They will be equipped with the means to gain greater fulfilment from their work by achieving more in their existing jobs and by obtaining the experience and skills that will further their careers.

Furthering development means noticing when formal training experiences or opportunities for on-the-job training can help someone. You should give your people time and space to learn new skills. Your role as a coach is particularly important. Every time you give somebody a new task to do you are creating a learning opportunity.

Provide leadership

Leadership is about treating people right. It helps them by giving a sense of direction and by providing support when necessary. Effective leadership means that people know where they are going and are guided on how to get there.

Get to know team members

You can't treat individual members of your team right unless you get to know them. You need to know their strengths and weaknesses, their ambitions and their concerns about work. Performance management systems that provide for regular review meetings between managers and their staff can help to do this. But it should be an everyday affair. The more you are in contact with your people the better you will get to know them. It's no good hiding in your office or behind a desk. You have to get out and talk to people. It's called management by walking about. It's one of the best ways of building good relationships.

Define expectations and ensure they are met

You treat people right when you make sure that they understand and accept what is expected of them – standards of performance and behaviour. You need to clarify roles, what needs to be achieved and how it is to be achieved. And this should be a matter for mutual agreement. You are not there as a manager simply to order people around. You want willing cooperation, not grudging submission.

But you have to ensure that the standards are met. If they are not, this is when you need to be firm. Treating people right is not about being soft with them. It is right to take a firm line if someone underperforms without good reason or misbehaves.

You must also remember that you have to earn the respect of your team members. Ten ways of doing this are set out below.

Gaining respect

1 Get things done well – impress people with your achievements.

2 Be professional – this means applying expertise in carrying out your work and acting responsibly at all times.

3 Engender trust – the firm belief that you can be relied on.

4 Respond promptly to requests for help or information.

5 Behave in a friendly and approachable manner.

6 Act firmly and with integrity, displaying honesty, probity, sincerity, fairness and morality.

7 Be polite, persistent and persuasive.

8 Deal calmly with people – never lose your temper.

9 Listen to people.

10 Take time to say thank you.

Endnote

1 Lawler, E E (2003) *Treat People Right*, Jossey-Bass, San Francisco

How to motivate people

Motivating people is the process of getting people to move in the direction you want them to go.

The organization as a whole can provide the context within which high levels of motivation can be achieved through reward systems and the provision of opportunities for learning and development. But individual managers still have a major part to play in deploying their own motivating skills so as to get individual members of their team to give of their best, and to make good use of the motivational systems and processes provided by the company.

To do this it is necessary to understand:

- the process of motivation;
- the different types of motivation;
- the basic concepts of motivation;
- the implications of motivation theory;
- approaches to motivation;
- the role of financial and non-financial rewards as motivators.

The process of motivation

Motivation is concerned with goal-directed behaviour. People are motivated to do something if they think it will be worth their while.

The process of motivation is initiated by someone recognizing an unsatisfied need. A goal is then established that, it is thought, will satisfy that need, and a course of action is determined that is expected to lead towards the attainment of that goal. This process is modelled in Figure 3.1.

Figure 3.1   The process of motivation

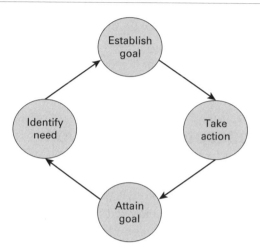

Basically, therefore, management and managers motivate people by providing means for them to satisfy their unsatisfied needs. This can be done by offering incentives and rewards for achievement and effort. But the needs of individuals and the goals associated with them vary so widely that it is difficult, if not impossible, to predict precisely how a particular incentive or reward will affect individual behaviour.

Types of motivation

Motivation at work can take two forms – intrinsic and extrinsic.

Intrinsic motivation takes place when individuals feel that their work is important, interesting and challenging and provides them with a reasonable degree of autonomy (freedom to act), opportunities to achieve and advance, and scope to use and develop their skills and abilities. It can be described as motivation by the work itself. It is not created by external incentives.

Extrinsic motivation occurs when things are done to or for people to motivate them. These include rewards, such as incentives, increased pay, praise, or promotion; and punishments, such as disciplinary action, withholding pay, or criticism. Extrinsic motivators can have an immediate and powerful effect, but it will not necessarily last long. The intrinsic motivators, which are concerned with the 'quality of working life' (a phrase and movement which emerged from this concept), are likely to have a deeper and longer-term effect because they are inherent in individuals and the work they do and are not imposed from outside in such forms as incentive pay.

Basic concepts of motivation

Extensive research has produced a number of motivation theories as described below. Remember that there is nothing so practical as a good theory, ie one based on systematic research which produces testable and proven explanations of behaviour which can be translated into effective practice.

Needs

Needs theory states that behaviour is motivated by unsatisfied needs. The key needs associated with work are those for achievement, recognition, responsibility, influence and personal growth.

Goals

Goal theory states that motivation will be increased if goal-setting techniques are used with the following characteristics:

- the goals should be specific;
- they should be challenging but reachable;
- they should be seen as fair and reasonable;
- individuals should participate fully in setting goals;
- feedback ensures that people feel pride and satisfaction from the experience of achieving a challenging but fair goal;
- feedback is used to gain commitment to even higher goals.

Reinforcement

Reinforcement theory suggests that success in achieving goals and rewards acts as a positive incentive and reinforces the successful behaviour, which is repeated the next time a similar need arises.

Expectancy theory

Expectancy theory states that motivation happens when individuals:

- feel able to change their behaviour;
- feel confident that a change in their behaviour will produce a reward;
- value the reward sufficiently to justify the change in behaviour.

The theory indicates that motivation is only likely when a clearly perceived relationship exists between performance and outcome, and the outcome is seen as a means of satisfying needs. This applies just as much to non-financial as to financial rewards. For example, if people want personal growth they will only be motivated by the opportunities available to them if they know what those opportunities are, if they know what they need to do to benefit from them (and can do it) and if the opportunities are worth striving for.

Expectancy theory explains why extrinsic motivation – for example, an incentive or bonus scheme – works only if the link between effort and reward is clear and the value of the reward is worth the effort. Such schemes should provide a clear line of sight between effort and reward. It also explains why intrinsic motivation arising from the work itself can sometimes be more powerful than extrinsic motivation. Intrinsic motivation outcomes are more under the control of individuals, who can place greater reliance on their past experiences to indicate the extent to which positive and advantageous results are likely to be obtained by their behaviour.

Implications of motivation theory

Motivation theory conveys two important messages. First, there are no simplistic solutions to increasing motivation. No single lever such as performance-related pay exists that is guaranteed to act as an effective motivator. This is because motivation is a complex process. It depends on:

- individual needs and aspirations, which are almost infinitely variable;
- both intrinsic and extrinsic motivating factors, and it is impossible to generalize on what the best mix of these is likely to be;
- expectations about rewards, which will vary greatly among individuals according to their previous experiences and perceptions of the reward system;
- the social context, where the influences of the organization culture, managers and co-workers can produce a wide variety of motivational forces that are difficult to predict and therefore to manage.

The second key message provided by motivation theory is the significance of expectations, goal-setting, feedback and reinforcement as motivating factors.

The implications of these messages are considered below.

Approaches to motivation

Creating the right climate

It is necessary, in general, to create a climate that will enable high motivation to flourish. This is a matter of managing the culture. The aims would be, first, to reinforce values concerning performance and competence; second, to emphasize norms (accepted ways of behaviour) relating to the ways in which people are managed and rewarded; and third, to demonstrate the organization's belief in empowerment – providing people with the scope and 'space' to exercise responsibility and use their abilities to the full. Without the right climate, quick fixes designed to improve motivation, such as performance-related pay, are unlikely to have much of an impact on overall organizational effectiveness, although they may work with some individuals.

Goal-setting, feedback and reinforcement

Goal-setting, feedback and reinforcement can all contribute to high motivation, and they are all within your control.

Managing expectations

It is necessary to manage expectations. No reward offered through an incentive, bonus or performance-related pay scheme will be effective as a motivator unless individuals believe it is worthwhile and can reasonably expect to obtain it through their own efforts. Similarly, people are more likely to be motivated if they know that their achievements will be recognized.

The implications of these approaches as they affect financial and non-financial reward policies and practices are set out below.

Financial rewards

Financial rewards need to be considered from three points of view:

- the effectiveness of money as a motivator;
- the reasons why people are satisfied or dissatisfied with their rewards;
- the criteria that should be used when developing a financial reward system.

Money and motivation

Money is important to people because it is instrumental in satisfying a number of their most pressing needs. It is significant not only because of what people can buy with it but also as a highly tangible method of recognizing their worth, thus improving their self-esteem and gaining the esteem of others.

Pay is the key to attracting people to join an organization, although job interest, career opportunities and the reputation of the organization will also be factors. Satisfaction with pay among existing employees is mainly related to feelings about equity and fairness. External and internal comparisons will form the basis of these feelings, which will influence their desire to stay with the organization.

Pay can motivate. As a tangible means of recognizing achievement, pay can reinforce desirable behaviour. Pay can also deliver messages on what the organization believes to be important. But to be effective, a pay-for-performance system has to meet the following stringent conditions:

- there must be a clear link between performance and reward;
- the methods used to measure performance should be perceived to be fair and consistent;
- the reward should be worth striving for;
- individuals should expect to receive a worthwhile reward if they behave appropriately.

As a manager you can make sure that the company's reward system is applied in your part of the organization in accordance with these principles.

Non-financial rewards

Dan Pink[1] states that there are three steps managers can take to improve motivation:

1 *Autonomy* – encourage people to set their own schedule and focus on getting work done, not how it is done.
2 *Mastery* – help people to identify the steps they can take to improve and ask them to identify how they will know they are making progress.

3 *Purpose* – when giving instructions explain the why as well as the how.

Such non-financial rewards are focused on the needs most people have, in varying degrees, for achievement, recognition, responsibility, influence and personal growth. You will be in a position to provide or withhold these rewards for those of your staff who are doing well or badly.

Achievement

The need for achievement is defined as the need for competitive success measured against a personal standard of excellence.

Achievement motivation can take place by providing people with the opportunity to perform and the scope in their jobs to use their skills and abilities.

Recognition

Recognition is one of the most powerful motivators. People need to know not only how well they have achieved their objectives or carried out their work but also that their achievements are appreciated.

Praise, however, should be given judiciously – it must be related to real achievements. And it is not the only form of recognition. Financial rewards, especially achievement bonuses awarded immediately after the event, are clear symbols of recognition to which tangible benefits are attached, and this is an important way in which mutually reinforcing processes of financial and non-financial rewards can operate. There are other forms of recognition such as long-service awards, status symbols of one kind or another, sabbaticals and trips abroad, all of which can be part of the total reward process.

Recognition is also provided by managers who listen to and act upon the suggestions of their team members and, importantly, acknowledge their contribution. Other actions that provide recognition include promotion, allocation to a high-profile project, enlargement of the job to provide scope for more interesting and rewarding work, and various forms of status or esteem symbols.

Responsibility

People can be motivated by being given more responsibility for their own work. This is essentially what empowerment is about and is in line with the concept of intrinsic motivation based on the content of the job. It is also related to the fundamental concept that individuals are motivated when they are provided with the means to achieve their goals.

The characteristics required in jobs if they are to be intrinsically motivating are that: first, individuals must receive meaningful feedback about their performance, preferably by evaluating their own performance and defining the feedback they require; second, the job must be perceived by individuals as requiring them to use abilities they value in order to perform the job effectively; and third, individuals must feel that they have a high degree of autonomy or self-control over setting their own goals and defining the paths to these goals.

Influence

People can be motivated by the drive to exert influence or to exercise power. David McClelland's[2] research established that, alongside the need for achievement, the need for power is a prime motivating force for managers, although the need for 'affiliation' – that is, warm, friendly relationships with others – is always present. The organization, through its policies for involvement, can provide motivation by putting people into situations where their views can be expressed, listened to and acted upon. This is another aspect of empowerment.

Personal growth

In Maslow's[3] hierarchy of needs, self-fulfilment or self-actualization is the highest need of all and is therefore the ultimate motivator. Maslow defines self-fulfilment as 'the need to develop potentialities and skills, to become what one believes one is capable of becoming'.

Ambitious and determined people will seek and find these opportunities for themselves, although the organization needs to clarify the scope for growth and development it can provide (if it does not, they will go away and grow elsewhere).

Increasingly, however, individuals at all levels in organizations, whether or not they are eaten up by ambition, recognize the importance of continually upgrading their skills and of progressively developing their careers. Many people now regard access to training as a key element in the overall reward package.

The availability of learning opportunities, the selection of individuals for high-prestige training courses and programmes, and the emphasis placed by the organization on the acquisition of new skills as well as the enhancement of existing ones, can all act as powerful motivators.

10 steps to achieving high levels of motivation

The following 10 steps need to be taken if you wish to achieve higher levels of motivation:

1 Set and agree demanding but achievable goals.

2 Provide feedback on performance.

3 Create expectations that certain behaviours and outputs will produce worthwhile rewards when people succeed but will result in penalties if they fail.

4 Design jobs that enable people to feel a sense of accomplishment, to express and use their abilities and to exercise their own decision-making powers.

5 Provide appropriate financial incentives and rewards for achievement (pay-for-performance).

6 Provide appropriate non-financial rewards such as recognition and praise for work well done.

7 Communicate to individuals and publicize generally the link between performance and reward – thus enhancing expectations.

8 Select and train team leaders who will exercise effective leadership and have the required motivating skills.

9 Give people guidance and training that will develop the knowledge, skills and competencies they need to improve their performance.

10 Show individuals what they have to do to develop their careers.

Endnotes

1 Pink, D H (2009) *Drive: The surprising truth about workplace motivation*, Riverhead Books, New York

2 McClelland, D C (1961) *The Achieving Society*, Van Nostrand, New York

3 Maslow, A (1954) *Motivation and Personality*, Harper & Row, New York

How to be a better leader   04

As a manager of people your role is to ensure that the members of your team give of their best to achieve the result you want. In other words, you are a leader – you set the direction and ensure that people follow you.

Leadership is the process of developing and communicating a vision for the future, motivating and guiding people and securing their engagement. Leaders know where they want to go and make sure that everyone in their teams goes in the same direction.

Some people believe that leadership is simply telling people what to do and then making them do it. This sort of autocratic approach may seem right but it doesn't work in the end. People do not like being coerced. It is preferable to regard a leader as someone who takes people where they want to go, while a great leader takes people where they don't necessarily want to go but ought to be.

To be a better leader you need to:

- know what leaders do;
- be aware of the different styles of leadership;
- appreciate the qualities that make a good leader;
- learn from examples of effective leaders;
- understand the reality of leadership;
- know how best to develop your leadership abilities.

What leaders do

The most convincing analysis of what leaders do was produced by John Adair.[1] He explained that the three essential roles of leaders are to:

1 *Define the task* – they make it quite clear what the group is expected to do.

2 *Achieve the task* – that is why the group exists. Leaders ensure that the group's purpose is fulfilled. If it is not, the result is frustration, disharmony, criticism and, eventually perhaps, disintegration of the group.

3 *Maintain effective relationships* – between themselves and the members of the group, and between the people within the group. These relationships are effective if they contribute to achieving the task. They can be divided into those concerned with the team and its morale and sense of common purpose, and those concerned with individuals and how they are motivated.

He suggested that demands on leaders are best expressed as three areas of need which they must satisfy. These are: 1) task needs – to get the job done; 2) individual needs – to harmonize the needs of the individual with the needs of the task and the group; and 3) group maintenance needs – to build and maintain team spirit. As shown in Figure 4.1, he modelled these demands as three interlocking circles.

This model indicates that the task, individual and group needs are interdependent. Satisfying task needs will also satisfy group and individual needs. Task needs, however, cannot be met unless attention is paid to individual and group needs, and looking after individual needs will also contribute to satisfying group needs and vice versa. There is a risk of becoming so task orientated that leaders ignore individual and group or team needs. It is just as dangerous to be too people orientated, focusing on meeting individual or group needs at the expense of the task. The best leaders are those who keep these three needs satisfied and in balance according to the demands of the situation.

Figure 4.1   John Adair's model of what leaders do

Leadership styles

Leadership style is the approach managers use in exercising leadership. It is sometimes called management style. There are many styles of leadership. To greater or lesser degrees, leaders can adopt any one of the styles described in Figure 4.2.

It should not be assumed that any one style is right in any circumstances. And there may be intermediate points between the extremes shown in Figure 4.2. There is no such thing as an ideal leadership style. It all depends. The factors affecting the degree to which a style is appropriate will be the type of organization, the nature of the task, the characteristics of the individuals in the leader's team and of the group as a whole, and, importantly, the personality of the leader.

Effective leaders are capable of flexing their style to meet the demands of the situation. Normally democratic leaders may have to shift into more of a directive mode when faced with a crisis, but they make clear what they are doing and why. Poor leaders change their style arbitrarily so that their team members are confused and do not know what to expect next.

Figure 4.2   Leadership styles

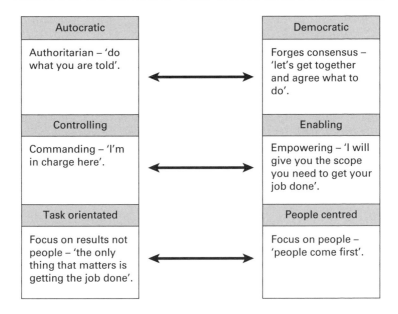

Good leaders may also flex their style when dealing with individual team members according to their characteristics. Some people need more positive direction than others. Others respond best if they are involved in decision-making with their boss. But there is a limit to the degree of flexibility that should be used. It is unwise to differentiate too much between the ways in which individuals are treated or to be inconsistent in one's approach.

What makes a good leader?

What makes a good leader? There is no universal answer to this question. But Lao-Tzu in the 6th century BC had a pretty good stab at it:

A leader is best

When people barely know that he exists.

Not so good when people obey and acclaim him.

Worst when they despise him.

Fail to honour people, they fail to honour you.

But a good leader who talks little,

When his work is done, his aim fulfilled,

They will all say, 'We did this ourselves.'

Effective leaders are confident and know what they need to do. They have the ability to take charge, convey their vision to their team, get their team members into action and ensure that they achieve their agreed goals. They are trustworthy, effective at influencing people and earn the respect of their team. They are aware of their own strengths and weaknesses and are skilled at understanding what will motivate their team members. They appreciate the advantages of consulting and involving people in decision-making. They can switch flexibly from one leadership style to another to meet the demands of different situations and people.

One of the key skills a leader or manager needs is an ability to analyse and read situations and to establish order and clarity in situations of ambiguity. Leaders need to have a sense of purpose, and an ability to influence others, interpret situations, negotiate and express their views, often in the face of opposition.

Research conducted by Penny Tamkin and colleagues[2] involving 260 in-depth interviews conducted with 77 business leaders from six high-profile organizations found that outstanding leaders:

- view things as a whole rather than compartmentalizing them;
- connect the parts through a guiding sense of purpose;
- are highly motivated to achieve excellence and are focused on organizational outcomes, vision and purpose;
- understand they cannot create performance themselves but are conduits for performance through their influence on others;
- watch themselves carefully and act consistently to achieve excellence through their interactions and their embodiment of the leadership role.

How do successful leaders do it?

Here are three examples.

Herb Kelleber – CEO, Southwest Airlines

Southwest is generally regarded as the world's most successful airline. It grew at a nearly constant annual rate of 10–15 per cent over its first 32 years of existence under the leadership of Herb Kelleber. He was described by *Fortune* magazine as 'perhaps the best CEO in America'.

As a leader, Herb Kelleber focused on relationships based on shared goals, shared knowledge and mutual respect. His theme was that tasks are achieved through the goodwill and support of others.

This goodwill and support originates in the leader seeing people as people, not just another resource for use in getting results. He expanded this as follows:

- Take the organizational pyramid.
- Turn it upside down on its point. Down here, at the bottom, you've got the people at headquarters. Up there, at the top, you've got the people who are out there in the field, on the front lines.
- They're the ones that make things happen, not us.

Bill George – Chairman and CEO of Medtronic (the biomedical engineering company)

Under his 12-year leadership the market capitalization of Medtronic increased at a rate of 35 per cent per year from US $1.1 billion to $60 billion.

He attributed this to what he called the practice of authentic leadership which he defined as follows:

- Authentic leaders genuinely want to serve others through their leadership.

- They are more interested in empowering the people they lead to make a difference than they are in power, money or prestige for themselves.
- They lead with purpose, meaning and values.
- They build enduring relationships with people.
- Others follow them because they know where they stand.
- They are consistent and self-disciplined.

Jack Welch – Chief Executive of General Electric

Jack Welch wrote that for a leader:

- Success is all about growing others.
- It's about making the people who work for you smarter, bigger and bolder.
- Nothing you do as an individual matters, except how you nurture and support your team and increase their self-confidence.
- Your success as a leader will come not from what you do, but from the reflected glory of your team.

The reality of leadership

The reality of leadership is that many first-line managers and supervisors are appointed or promoted to their posts with some idea, possibly, of what their managerial or supervisory duties are, but with no appreciation of the leadership skills they need. They see their role as being to tell people what to do and then make sure that they do it. They may focus on getting the job done and neglect everything else.

However, the better ones will rely on their know-how (authority goes to the person who knows), their quiet confidence and their cool, analytical approach to dealing with problems. Any newly appointed leader or individual who is progressing to a higher level of leadership will benefit from a leadership development programme which will help them to understand and apply the skills they need.

Leadership checklists

Task

- What needs to be done and why?
- What results have to be achieved and by when?
- What problems have to be overcome?
- To what extent are these problems straightforward?
- Is there a crisis situation?
- What has to be done now to deal with the crisis?
- What are these priorities?
- What pressures are likely to be exerted?

Individuals

- What are their strengths and weaknesses?
- What are likely to be the best ways of motivating them?
- What tasks are they best at doing?
- Is there scope to increase flexibility by developing new skills?
- How well do they perform in achieving targets and performance standards?
- To what extent can they manage their own performance and development?
- Are there any areas where there is a need to develop skill or competence?
- How can I provide them with the sort of support and guidance that will improve their performance?

Teams

- How well is the team organized?
- Does the team work well together?

- How can the commitment and motivation of the team be achieved?
- What is the team good and not so good at doing?
- What can I do to improve the performance of the team?
- Are team members flexible – capable of carrying out different tasks?
- To what extent can the team manage its own performance?
- Is there scope to empower the team so that it can take on greater responsibility for setting standards, monitoring performance and taking corrective action?
- Can the team be encouraged to work together to produce ideas for improving performance?

A 10-point plan for developing leadership skills

1   Understand what is meant by leadership.

2   Appreciate the different leadership styles available.

3   Assess what you believe to be your fundamental leadership style.

4   Get other people, colleagues and indeed your own team members to tell you what they think your leadership style is and how well it works.

5   In the light of this information, consider what you need to do and can do to modify your style, bearing in mind that you have to go on being the same person. In other words, your style should still be a natural one.

6   Think about the typical situations and problems with which you are confronted as a leader. Will your leadership style, modified as necessary, be appropriate for all of them? If not, can you think of any of those situations where a different style would have been better? If so, think about what you need to do to be able to flex your style as necessary without appearing to be inconsistent to your team.

7 Examine the various explanations of the qualities that make a good leader and assess your own performance using the checklists set out above. Decide what you need to do – what you can do – about any weaknesses.

8 Think about or observe any managers you know whom you have worked for or with.

9 Assess each of them in terms of the qualities set out in the leadership skills checklists above.

10 Consider what you can learn from them about effective and less effective leadership behaviours. In the light of this, assess where you could usefully modify your own leadership behaviours.

Endnotes

1 Adair, J (1973) *The Action-Centred Leader*, McGraw-Hill, London

2 Tamkin, P, Pearson, G, Hirsh, W and Constable, S (2010) *Exceeding Expectation: The principles of outstanding leadership*, The Work Foundation, London

How to be an engaging manager   05

Engaging managers achieve high levels of engagement amongst the members of their teams. Engagement takes place when people at work:

- are interested in and positive, even excited, about their jobs;
- will go the extra mile to get their jobs done to the best of their ability by exercising 'discretionary effort' – where necessary they are prepared to do more than is normally expected of them, things that are 'not in their job description';
- are committed to the organization and its values – they believe that the organization is a 'great place in which to work', that what it does is worthwhile, that it behaves to its customers, employees and the public at large in an ethical manner and that they want to remain part of it.

Engaged employees achieve higher levels of performance and are more innovative than others, are more likely to want to stay with their employers, feel better about their work and the organization and believe that they cope well with their workload.

What you can do to increase levels of engagement

Research by Lewis and colleagues in 2012 for the Chartered Institute of Personnel and Development[1] resulted in the following list of what an engaging manager does:

- trusts and involves employees;
- helps to develop employees' careers;
- gives positive feedback and praise and rewards good work;
- shows concern for employees;
- is there when needed;
- has a positive approach, leads by example;
- treats employees fairly;
- helps and advises employees;
- sets clear goals and defines what is expected;
- ensures resources are available to meet workload and individual interests;
- understands and explains processes and procedures.

Research conducted by Dilys Robinson in 2013 for the Institute for Employment Studies[2] found that managers who achieved high levels of engagement amongst their team members contributed to their teams' success by being very clear about what they expected their teams to achieve, thus giving them focus and a sense of purpose. Engaging managers were also good at giving feedback and encouraged an open culture in which team members felt free to admit mistakes and ask for help. Suggestions for improvement were made in a positive way. Here are some comments made by employees about their managers:

> ... I think it's just the way she approaches things, as if she has confidence in your ability. She'll tell you if you're not on track... so she doesn't let you go gaily down the road, off on the wrong track.

> He gives a steer. If you need help he gives it; otherwise, he trusts you to get on with it.

> She keeps us informed all the time how well we're all doing separately and then as a team together. All the time, each week she says we're doing well or we're not doing well or what we need to do to improve.

> As soon as she came in, she had a plan of action, saying, well I want to sit in when you're doing reviews, your team talks. I want to see how

you address your agents, I want to see how you facilitate a meeting for example... she's given us hints and tips, a way we can move forward, what we're doing well, what we can continue, what we can do differently the next time.

Endnotes

1 Lewis, R, Donaldson-Feilder, E and Tharani, T (2012) Management Competencies for Enhancing Employee Engagement, CIPD, London

2 Robinson, D (2013) The engaging manager and sticky situations, *Institute for Employment Studies* [online] http://www.employment-studies.co.uk/system/files/resources/files/493.pdf [accessed 8 November 2016]

How to manage performance 06

One of your most important responsibilities as a manager is to ensure that the members of your team achieve high levels of performance. Many organizations have a formal performance management system that is supposed to help managers fulfil these responsibilities and the traditional approach is described in the next section of this chapter. In the absence of such a system, managers have to manage performance by themselves, as considered in the rest of this chapter. But even when there is a formal system it often fails to operate properly and managers have to do the best they can on their own.

The traditional performance management system

The focal point of the traditional system is an annual formal meeting between managers and their individual team members to review or appraise performance over the year (some organizations have meetings twice a year). During the meeting, progress in achieving the objectives or goals set at the beginning of the year is reviewed, individuals are given feedback on their performance and they are usually rated on a scale, typically five points such as a = outstanding, b = good, c = fully satisfactory, d = fairly satisfactory, and e = unsatisfactory. What is called a forced distribution system may be used to ensure that ratings follow an acceptable and consistent pattern throughout the organization. This would require managers to distribute ratings to a pattern such as a = 10 per cent, b = 20 per cent, c = 40 per cent, d = 20 per cent and e = 10 per cent. The ratings may be used to inform performance pay decisions or indicate potential for promotion. At the end of the meeting, new objectives are set for the coming year. Ideally, there is also a discussion on performance development needs. The manager completes a form on paper or on a computer, ticking the appropriate boxes, and this is kept by the HR (human resources) department.

But this approach is fundamentally flawed. The following comments were made recently by the Institute for Employment Studies on the basis of their research:

> Managers and employees in the IES study not only found the PM process complex and bureaucratic, they felt this completely masked its fundamental purpose. The commonest criticism by both managers and employees was that it was a box-ticking or form-filling exercise... The loudest message from HR and senior managers is that of the need to get the forms filled in on time – a message about administrative compliance. So again, in a real sense, HR is asking for form-filling, so should not be surprised when managers say it feels like form-filling!

A manager interviewed during the research said:

> Performance management is seen as something you do to keep HR quiet. It's seen as owned by HR, not about how you manage people properly.

Such criticisms have been made by many other commentators and there has been a backlash against the traditional approach. This has involved the abolition of the formal annual review meeting and its replacement by more frequent and informal conversations about performance and development as described below. Reliance is now placed more on developing the skills of managers in holding such conversations rather than compelling them to follow a bureaucratic regime. Some large organizations have also abandoned rating.

A better approach to managing performance

Managing performance is what managers do all the time. It is not something they only do in an annual meeting as part of a performance management system. It is about good management, not ticking boxes on a form. Good managers manage performance by ensuring that their team members understand what they are expected to achieve, work with their teams to review performance against those expectations, provide regular feedback on results and agree with individuals what needs to be done to improve performance and develop knowledge and skills.

In her research into the characteristics of successful managers for the Institute for Employment Studies, Dilys Robinson[1] identified five key factors affecting how they managed performance:

1 Managers were very clear in their expectations, which gave a focus and a sense of purpose to their teams.

2 Managers described effectively how their teams contributed to the organization's overall purpose and direction. This made the team feel valued and enabled them to articulate clearly how they, as individuals and as a team, helped the organization to achieve its objectives.

3 Managers were good at seeing that team members knew what they were supposed to be doing. But the managers did not prescribe activities, go into great detail, or 'micro manage' in any way. Rather, they explained the task, its intended outcome and why the team was being asked to do it, and then allowed people to get on with it.

4 Managers set clear quality and behavioural standards, so their teams knew the level at which they should be operating. The teams appreciated the way in which the managers acted as role models by following these standards themselves.

5 Managers were aware of how individuals and the team as a whole were doing, and gave frequent feedback (both positive and, when things were not going so well, remedial). Team members appreciated the timely and frequent feedback they received.

Here are some comments by managers she interviewed about how they managed performance:

> So, the key for me is just one-to-one time, and they know what they're aiming for, and we talk about it regularly.

So it never really gets to the situation where there's like a really great big formal sit-down to say let's review everything you've done.

I think it's regular dialogue... at least once a fortnight for an extended period of time, just one to one and just about them and the work they're doing and what's going on... just so that I understand what they're doing and so I can give a bit of a steer or give them a bit of coaching if they need some coaching; help them if they want some help and support.

Every week I have a one-to-one session with people who work for me. And it's half an hour; it's the opportunity to talk things over with people. I say to people it's your time with me. But, to be honest, it's not just that; it's me getting to talk to them.

The best way to manage performance is to act like this rather than comply with the bureaucratic requirements of a typical performance management system. These managers are managing performance, not operating a system.

Managing underperformers

In spite of all your efforts to enhance performance, it is almost inevitable that you will have to deal sometime with someone who is underperforming. Here are 10 tips on how to do this:

1   Identify the areas of underperformance – be specific.

2   Establish the causes of poor performance – is it because the individual is in the wrong job, or lacks the necessary skills, or has been given insufficient support and guidance from his or her team leader, or is simply not trying hard enough?

3   Adopt a problem-solving approach to dealing with the situation – obtain agreement on the actions required by the individual and/or by the manager.

4   Ensure that the necessary resources are provided to enable the problem to be overcome.

5 Provide coaching.

6 Provide additional training.

7 Consider reallocation of duties.

8 Monitor progress and provide feedback.

9 Provide additional guidance as required.

10 As a last resort, invoke a capability or disciplinary procedure, starting with an informal warning.

Endnote

1 Robinson, D (2013) The engaging manager and sticky situations, *Institute for Employment Studies* [online] http://www.employment-studies.co.uk/system/files/resources/files/493.pdf [accessed 8 November 2016]

How to handle difficult situations with people   07

We all have to deal with people problems from time to time. We come across difficult individuals who behave negatively. We have to give people bad news and we have to conduct challenging conversations. We may have to discipline someone, even, in extreme cases, dismiss them. If we don't handle them well the result is frustration, anger and other counterproductive activities.

Handling difficult people

Why people are difficult

When considering why people can be difficult it is worth remembering that they may be equally convinced that it is you who is being difficult, not them. People respond in kind, so when assessing the situation, you have to ask yourself whether the problem is caused by your behaviour rather than theirs.

There are many reasons that people can be difficult (whether it is you or them). Here are some of them:

- a fundamental disagreement about what they are expected to do or how they are expected to do it;
- rivalry;
- a real or imagined slight;
- arrogant behaviour – or behaviour perceived as arrogant;

- a feeling that they are not valued for their contribution or themselves;
- frustrated ambition – where the cause of frustration is attributed to you;
- not being given the attention they believe they deserve;
- not being able to get their own way;
- lack of trust;
- insecurity;
- concern about the impact of change;
- too much pressure – real or perceived.

In addition, there is the Dr Fell reason for being difficult:

> I do not love thee, Dr Fell,
>
> The reason why I cannot tell;
>
> But this I know, I know full well,
>
> I do not love thee, Dr Fell.

The last reason is, of course, the hardest to deal with. An attempt can be made to handle the other instances, although success will depend on how much effort you put into it, and will be limited or delayed if the causes of disagreement are deeply seated or are based more on prejudice than on reason (which is often the case).

10 approaches to handling difficult people

1   Anticipate problems as far as possible.

2   Act quickly. One notable finding of the research conducted by Dilys Robinson[1] into managers who achieved high levels of engagement amongst their team members was that engaging managers typically act quite quickly in response to displays

of undesirable behaviour, partly to nip it in the bud, but also because they did not want the rest of the team to be influenced. As one manager put it:

> I've learnt to tackle issues quickly, not prevaricate. It's uncomfortable to tackle things head on but it's best. I need to trust my own style and judgement. I've learnt not to try to bury things and hope they'll go away.

3 Subject your own behaviour to close scrutiny. Is it caused by something you have done?

4 Analyse the possible cause or causes.

5 Try to reach agreement that a problem exists. Use questioning to identify what it is and how it could be solved and agree an action plan.

6 Discuss the issue with the individual. A joint problem-solving approach is best, when both parties spend some time in analysing the cause of the difficulty so that agreement can be reached on what they can both do about it. As a line manager said to Dilys Robinson:

> With some difficult people, it is about... letting them know when they're being difficult and sitting down and talking them through... and making sure that I've got all the evidence up my sleeve to be able to have that conversation in a very robust way...

7 Stand your ground when dealing with aggressive people.

8 Always be calm. Losing your temper with someone who is angry gets you nowhere.

9 Try to reason with the difficult person. But if he or she is too angry or upset to listen, it may be best to withdraw temporarily, with words to the effect that time is needed to reflect on this situation.

10 Think carefully about the words you use. Try to limit your contribution and let the other person have his or her say.

Giving people bad news

Dilys Robinson found that in giving bad news, engaging managers acted honestly and openly and refused to dissemble or lie to their teams. Here are some comments made to her by line managers:

> You have to be as open as possible, and explain the rationale.

> My experience is to be upfront, to give bad news, to put it in context, clearly... my commitment is to give them the information and context to make that decision for themselves... people would rather have bad news when there's bad news to give, rather than have managers who string them along.

> I come straight out with it. There's no point trying to soften the blow, you need to be open and frank. I try to help people through the acceptance stage once the news is delivered, by helping them through the process and increasing their understanding.

> I've learnt to tackle issues quickly, not prevaricate. It's uncomfortable to tackle things head on but its best. I need to trust my own style and judgement. I've learnt not to try to bury things and hope they'll go away.

Handling challenging conversations

Many managers find it difficult to have conversations or hold meetings with individuals about performance issues. In advance, these can look difficult and in practice they can be challenging if the manager wants to achieve desired changes or improvements in performance. They can be even more challenging in prospect if it is feared that unpleasantness may occur in the shape of lack of cooperation or outright hostility, or in practice when this happens in spite of efforts to prevent it. The following is a 12-point guide to handling challenging conversations.

1   Don't wait until a formal review meeting. Have a quiet word at the first sign that something is going wrong.

2   Get the facts in advance – what happened, when and why?

3   Plan the meeting on the basis of the facts and what is known about the individual. Define what is to be achieved.

4   Set the right tone from the start of the meeting – adopt a calm, measured, deliberate but friendly approach.

5   Begin the conversation by explaining the purpose of the meeting, indicating to the individual what the issue is and giving specific examples.

6   Focus on the issue and not the person.

7   Ask for an explanation. Ask unloaded questions to clarify the issues and explore them together.

8   Allow people to have their say and listen to them.

9   Keep an open mind and don't jump to conclusions.

10   Acknowledge the individual's position and any mitigating circumstances.

11   Ask the employee for proposals to resolve the situation, discuss the options and as far as possible agree on action by the individual, the manager or jointly.

12   If agreement cannot be reached, managers may have to define the way forward, with reasons – they are in charge!

Handling disciplinary problems

If all else fails and you have not been able to solve a performance or behaviour problem you may have to invoke your firm's disciplinary procedure if it has one. Such procedures provide for a staged process starting with an informal warning followed, if there is no improvement, with a formal written warning and, as a last resort, a final warning indicating that disciplinary action will be taken if there is no change. Whether or not there is a disciplinary procedure, managers may find themselves having to conduct an interview. If this is the case, make sure that you have got all the facts and then use the following approach:

1 Give employees notice that the interview is going to take place so that they can be prepared and can get a representative to accompany them.

2 Arrange for a colleague to be present to help conduct the interview and to take notes.

3 State the complaint to the employee, giving chapter and verse and giving supporting statements from other people involved where appropriate.

4 Allow employees to give their side of the story and call any supporting witnesses.

5 Question employees and their witnesses and allow them to do the same.

6 Allow time for a general discussion on the issues raised and any other relevant issues.

7 Give employees an opportunity to have a final say and mention any mitigating circumstances.

8 Sum up the points emerging from the meeting as you see them, but allow employees to comment on them and be prepared to amend your summary.

9 Adjourn the meeting so that you can consider your decision on the basis of what came out in the interview. It is best not to announce the decision during the initial meeting. The adjournment may be only half an hour or so in a straightforward case. It could be longer in a more complex case.

10 Reconvene the meeting and announce your decision.

11 Confirm your decision in writing.

Dismissing people

You should always try to help someone to improve, and if there are performance problems you should go conscientiously through each stage of the capability or disciplinary procedure.

Unfortunately, however, you may still find yourself unable to avoid having to dismiss a person because of a continuing failure to meet an acceptable standard. The following are the points to bear in mind if this happens:

- Come straight to the point. Tell the person within 30 seconds of starting the interview that he or she has to go.

- Be clear about shortcomings, quoting chapter and verse, but avoid 'badmouthing' the individual.

- Don't say you're sorry. If you are certain that this is the right course of action, you have nothing to apologize for.

- Make it plain that, as far as you are concerned, the decision is irrevocable but that the employee has the right to appeal.

- Ensure that you have a witness in case there is an appeal or legal action.

- Carry out the dismissal on a Friday.

- Take steps to ensure that the individual does not have access to a computer or confidential information after dismissal, but do not arrange for him or her to be 'marched off the premises', as sometimes happens.

- Be aware of the legal issues such as the possibility of a claim for unfair dismissal if you have not followed a fair disciplinary procedure or do not have just cause for your action.

Endnote

1 Robinson, D (2013) The engaging manager and sticky situations, *Institute of Employment Studies* [online] http://www.employment-studies.co.uk/system/files/resources/files/493.pdf [accessed 8 November 2016]

How to provide feedback 08

What is feedback?

Feedback is the provision of information to people on how they have performed in terms of the results they have achieved and how they achieved those results.

Why is feedback important?

Feedback lets people know how they stand and what they can do to improve their performance. It plays a key role, along with goal-setting, in the self-regulation of performance. Feedback focuses attention on performance goals that are important to the organization, helps discover errors, maintains direction in achieving goals, influences new goals, provides information on performance capabilities and on how much more effort/energy is needed to reach goals, and provides positive reinforcement for goal accomplishments.

The importance of feedback has been described by Charles Lee[1] as follows.

The use of feedback in reviewing and developing performance

Performance conversations should include a two-way exchange to ensure that the employee fully understands what is good, what is bad, and why the good performance is good and the bad is bad. With accurate descriptions of the nuances of performance the employee can better understand how his or her past actions or activities affected performance outcomes and how future efforts are likely to contribute to future performance. Accurate descriptions or diagnoses of performance are crucial for understanding and improvements are possible only through timely feedback.

The longer the gap between performance events and performance feedback, the greater the challenge of remembering with clarity the character and quality of the performance events... two semi-annual performance conversations or one annual one cannot manage performance alone. They might be effective in documenting some performance parameters but they are not likely to be effective in managing, regulating and improving performance. Good supervision with ample feedback is good performance management.

What is meant by positive and negative feedback?

Feedback is positive and helpful when it recognizes success and constructive when it identifies areas for improvement that can lead to effective action. It is negative and unhelpful when perceived failings are dwelt on as matters for blame. A positive approach is to treat mistakes or errors of judgement as opportunities for learning so that they are less likely to be repeated in the future.

What are the requirements for successful feedback?

- Provide positive and constructive feedback.
- Build feedback into the job – clarify key performance indicators.
- Provide feedback on actual events at the time – base it on factual evidence.

- Deliver the feedback.
- Describe, don't judge.
- Be non-threatening.
- Address performance issues but do not make it personal.
- Refer to and define specific behaviours.
- Define good work or behaviour.
- Ask questions.
- Select key issues.
- Cover how the task was tackled, don't focus just on the results.
- Ensure feedback leads to action.

Approaches to feedback

Feedback will be most effective if it is delivered as soon after the event as possible when the situation is fresh in everyone's memory and it will make the most impact.

It should not be postponed until a formal end-of-year performance review. If action is not taken quickly the employee could be misled by being given the impression that there is no problem and may be denied the chance to improve or put things right.

Managers should focus only on *what* has been achieved, not with *how* it was achieved.

Never make personal attacks. Always base the message on recent factual evidence and offer facts rather than opinions.

Endnote

1 Lee, C D (2005) Rethinking the goals of your performance management system, *Employment Relations Today*, **32** (3), pp 53–60

PART TWO
Developing people

How to develop 09 people

People learn and develop mainly from experience which means that most development takes place in the workplace. But they need support and help. This is your job as a manager. You need to appreciate the importance of investing in people and take the steps required to develop them, as explained in this chapter.

Investing in people

The chairman of an advertising firm once said that his 'inventory goes up and down in the lift'. His prime resource – his working capital – was people. The same applies in any other sort of organization. Money matters, but the human beings who work there matter even more.

If you want to take a pragmatic view of people, regard them as an investment. They cost money to acquire and maintain and they should provide a return on that outlay; their value increases as they become more effective in their jobs and capable of taking on greater responsibility. In accounting terms, people may be treated like any other asset on the balance sheet, taking into account acquisition costs and their increasing value as they gain experience.

10 steps to develop people at work

The following are 10 ways in which you can develop your staff:

1   Analyse what you expect job holders to know and to be able to do. If necessary, seek help from specialized trainers to carry out this analysis.

2 Determine the standards of performance required for each of the jobs you control.

3 Ensure that the individuals concerned know what is expected of them.

4 Review with these individuals their performance so that agreement can be reached on any gaps to be filled between what they can do and what they should be able to do.

5 Every time you give someone an instruction, treat it as a learning opportunity. Encourage individuals to tell you how they would do the job. If they get it wrong, help them to work out the best way for themselves, progressively giving them less guidance so they learn to stand on their own feet.

6 Don't expect too much. People can take time to learn something (the learning curve). They need to understand what they have to do and to acquire and practise the skills they need. Remember that people learn at different rates – don't expect everyone to progress at the same rate. But do require learners to improve at a pace that matches their natural aptitudes. Only bear down hard on people if they are clearly not trying – without any excuse.

7 Train and develop by example. Give people the opportunity to learn from the way you do things. Remember the truth of the saying that managers learn best how to manage by managing under a good manager. This principle applies equally well to other categories of job holders.

8 Remember that the prime responsibility for training and developing your staff rests with you. Your results depend on their abilities and skills. You neglect your training responsibilities at your peril. And you must not rely on the learning and development function to do it for you. It can provide advice and help but cannot replace your capacity to train on the job.

9 Plan the training for your staff in accordance with a regular review of their training needs.

10 Remember that one of the best ways in which you can develop your staff is by coaching them, as described in Chapter 10.

How to coach   10
people

Coaching is a key part of a manager's job. You need to know why it is important, what it entails and how to do it.

What is coaching?

Coaching is a personal (usually one-to-one), on-the-job approach that can be used by managers to help people develop their skills and levels of competence. As a manager, you are there to get results through people; this means that you have a personal responsibility for ensuring that they acquire and develop the skills they need. Other people in the shape of coaching, training and management development specialists may help, but because by far the best way of learning is on the job, the onus is mainly on you.

The need for coaching

The need for coaching may arise from formal or informal performance reviews but opportunities for coaching will emerge during normal day-to-day activities. Every time you delegate a new task to someone, a coaching opportunity is created to help the individual learn any new skills or techniques that are needed to do the job. Every time you provide feedback to an individual after a task has been completed, there is an opportunity to help that individual do better next time.

The approach to coaching

Coaching can be carried out informally on the spot – it is not essential to set up special coaching sessions. Coaching should be regarded as a normal part of your job and accepted as such by the members of your team.

Aims of coaching

The aims of coaching are to:

- help people to become aware of how well they are doing, where they need to improve and what they need to learn;
- put controlled delegation into practice; in other words, managers can delegate new tasks or enlarged areas of work, provide guidance as necessary on how the tasks or work should be carried out and monitor performance in doing the work;
- get managers and individuals to use whatever situations arise as learning opportunities;
- enable guidance to be provided on how to carry out specific tasks as necessary, but always on the basis of helping people to learn rather than spoon-feeding them with instructions on what to do and how to do it.

The coaching sequence

Coaching can be carried out in the following stages:

1 Identify the areas of knowledge, skills or capabilities where learning needs to take place to qualify people to carry out the task, provide for continuous development, enhance transferable skills or improve performance.

2 Ensure that the person understands and accepts the need to learn.

3 Discuss with the person what needs to be learnt and the best way to undertake the learning.

4 Get the person to work out how they can manage their own learning while identifying where they will need help from you or someone else.

5 Provide encouragement and advice to the person in pursuing the self-learning programme.

6 Provide specific guidance as required where the person needs your help.

7 Agree how progress should be monitored and reviewed.

PART THREE
Management skills

How to control   11

Basically, you are seeking to control two areas – input and output – and the relationship between them, which is productivity or performance. All managers will know Murphy's two laws: if anything can go wrong, it will; and of the things that can't go wrong, some will.

The aim of good control is to protect your plans from the operation of these laws as far as possible, to detect trouble spots before they erupt, to prevent those accidents that are just waiting to happen. Prevention is better than cure.

Essentials of control

Control is relative. It does not deal with absolutes, only with the difference between good and not-so-good performance.

The basis of control is measurement. It depends on accurate information about what is being achieved. This is then compared with what should have been achieved and with what has been achieved in the past. But that is only a starting point. Good control also identifies responsibility and points the way to action.

Effective control

If you want to exercise good control you need to:

- plan what you aim to achieve;
- measure regularly what has been achieved;
- compare actual achievements with the plan;
- take action to exploit opportunities revealed by this information or to correct deviations from the plan.

Note that control is not only a matter of putting things right. It also has a positive side – getting more or better things done on the basis of information received.

Problems of control

A good control system is not easy to set up. There are two basic problems:

1 How to set appropriate and fair targets, standards and budgets. (This may be difficult where the scope for quantification is limited or if circumstances make forecasts unreliable.) Note that targets are good to have, within reason, but too many can cause resentment, confusion and focusing on producing the right numbers rather than doing the right things.

2 How to decide what information is crucial for control purposes and design reports that clearly convey that information to the people who need it and can use it to point the way to action. Too many control systems generate a surfeit of indigestible data that go to the wrong people and are not acted upon. You can have too little information, but there is also such a thing as information overkill. There is, moreover, a tendency for some people to report good results and cover up poor ones. In any case, the figures may not tell the whole story.

Achieving good control

There are seven steps to take if you want to achieve good control:

1 Decide what you want to control – focus on the key result areas.

2 Decide how you are going to measure and review performance.

3 Ensure that only a limited number of key controls are necessary – too many causes confusion and limits performance.

4 Use ratio analysis to make comparisons and to identify variations and problems (but take care with ratios as suggested in Chapter 56).

5 Set up a control system which is comprehensive but not too elaborate.

6 Use targets carefully – don't rely on them as the only control mechanism.

7 Manage by exception.

Controlling inputs and outputs

In controlling input and output, and hence productivity, an overview is essential. It is no good concentrating on inputs, mainly expressed as costs, unless you look at the benefits arising from these expenditures and the effectiveness with which the costs have been incurred. Cost–benefit and cost-effectiveness studies are an essential part of the control process.

Input control

When you control inputs you should aim to measure and assess the performance of:

- *Money* – its productivity, flow, liquidity and conservation. This involves four requirements:

  1 You need to know what return you are getting on investments compared with the return you want.

  2 You should ensure that you have the cash and working capital to run the business. Cash-flow analysis is vital. One of the golden rules of financial management is 'cash in must exceed cash out'.

  3 You must conserve and provide the money needed to finance future trading and development projects and for capital investment.

  4 Management has to know how effectively its financial resources are being used to produce goods, services and profits, and this requires continuous and close attention to the control of direct and indirect costs and overheads generally.

- *People* – the effectiveness of the people you employ in terms of their quality and performance.
- *Materials* – their availability, condition, convertibility and waste.
- *Equipment* – machine utilization and capability.

Output control

Quantitative control measures – the units produced or sold, the amount of services provided, the sales turnover obtained and the profits achieved. Key performance measures will vary between organizations. You need to determine through analysis which are the crucial indicators of success or failure.

Qualitative control measures – the level of service provided by an organization (eg a public corporation) or by a non-productive department within an organization (eg HR). It is more difficult to select valid performance measures in these areas, but the attempt should be made.

Control systems

What you need from a control system

Your basic requirement is reports that clearly identify areas of good and bad performance so that appropriate action can be taken.

At higher levels, 'exception reporting' should be adopted so that significant deviations, on which action should be taken, can be highlighted. Overall summaries of performance against plan and of trends will also be necessary at this level, but these may disguise significant underlying deviations that would be pointed out in an exception report.

The reports themselves should:

- contain measurements that are accurate, valid and reliable, and that permit a direct and easy comparison between planned and actual performance;

- analyse trends, comparing one period's performance with that of the previous period or of the same period the previous year and, where appropriate, summarizing the year-to-date position;
- be given to the person who is responsible for the activity concerned;
- arrive promptly, in time to allow the necessary action to be taken;
- provide succinct explanations of any deviations from plan.

Measurements

Measurement is a good thing, but all figures need to be treated with caution. They may conceal more than they reveal. The weaknesses to look for are:

- *Non-representative reporting* – data selected that do not cover the key issues, disguise unfavourable results or overemphasize favourable performance.
- *Not comparing like with like* – the 'apples and pears syndrome'. For example, a trend or projection that does not take account of changing or new factors that have altered or will alter the situation since the base data were collected.
- *Not starting from a common base* – this is a variant on the 'like with like' problem. Trend comparisons should be related to a common base in terms both of the period and the elements covered by the information.
- *Misleading averages* – averages do not always tell you the whole story. They may conceal significant extremes in performance.
- *Unintentional errors* – simple mistakes in calculation, presentation or observation.
- *Measurements out of context* – almost any single measure is influenced by, or inseparable from, other measures. Figures in isolation may not mean very much. You have to know about relationships and underlying influences.

Management by exception

Management by exception is a system that rings alarm bells only when the manager's attention is needed. The principle was invented by the father of scientific management, Frederick Taylor. In 1911 he wrote in *Principles of Scientific Management*:[1]

> Under the exception principle the manager should receive only condensed, summarized and invariably comparative reports covering, however, all of the elements entering into the management and even these summaries should all be carefully gone over by an assistant before they reach the manager, and have all the exceptions to the past averages or standards pointed out, both the especially good and the especially bad exceptions, thus giving him in a few minutes a full view of progress which is being made, or the reverse, and leaving him free to consider the broader lines of policy and to study the character and fitness of the important men under him.

Management by exception frees the boss to concentrate on the issues that matter. It gives the subordinate more scope to get on with his or her work while knowing that events out of the ordinary will be reported upwards.

Deciding what constitutes an exception is a useful exercise in itself. It means selecting the key events and measures that will show up good, bad or indifferent results and indicate whether or not performance is going according to plan.

The chosen indicators or ratios can be studied so that the significance of changes or trends is readily understood. More important, the possible causes of deviations can be analysed and kept in mind. Investigations can then be quickly launched in the right direction and swift remedial action can be taken.

Most of us have come across the boss or manager who seems to have the almost magic facility for studying a mass of figures and immediately spotting the one really important deviation or the item that does not ring true. It sometimes seems to be pure instinct, but of course it is not. Such managers are practising the art of management by exception, even if they never call it by that name. Their experience and analytical powers have told them what constitutes normal performance. But they can spot something out of the ordinary at a thousand paces. They know what the key indicators are and they look for them, hard. This is a skill that anyone can develop. And the effort of acquiring it is well worthwhile.

Endnote

1 Taylor, F (1911) *Principles of Scientific Management*, Harper & Row, New York

How to coordinate 12

Coordinating – 'achieving unity of effort' – covers all actions taken by managers leading to the achievement of a result by a number of different parties. It is not a separate function of a manager and the concept of coordination does not describe a particular set of operations.

Coordination is required because individual actions need to be integrated. Some activities must follow one another in sequence. Others must go on at the same time and in the same direction in order to finish together.

Approaches to coordination

Obviously, you can achieve good coordination by getting people to work well together. This means integrating their activities, communicating well, exercising leadership and team building (all subjects covered in individual chapters). But you should also pay attention to the specific techniques discussed below.

Planning

Coordinating should take place before the event rather than after it. Planning is the first step. This means deciding what should be done and when. It is a process of dividing the total task into a number of sequenced or related sub-tasks. Then you work out priorities and timescales.

Organizing

You know what should be done. You then decide who does it.

When you divide work between people you should avoid breaking apart those tasks that are linked together and that you cannot separate cleanly from each other.

Your biggest problem will be deciding where the boundaries between distinct but related activities should be. If the boundary is either too rigid or insufficiently well defined, you may have coordination problems. Don't rely too much upon the formal organization as defined in job descriptions, charts and manuals. If you do, you will induce inflexibility and set up communication barriers, and these are fatal to coordination.

The informal organization that exists in all companies can help coordination. When people work together they develop a system of social relationships that cut across formal organizational boundaries. They create a network of informal groups that tend to discipline themselves. This frees management from detailed supervision and control and leaves it more time for planning, problem-solving and the overall monitoring of performance.

Delegating

The informal organization can help, but you still need to delegate work to individuals in a way that ensures they know what is expected of them and are aware of the need to liaise with others to achieve a coordinated result.

The art is to make everyone concerned understand the points on which they must link up with other people and the time in which such actions have to be completed. You should not have to tell people to coordinate; they should do so almost automatically. This they will do if you delegate not only specific tasks but also the job of working with others.

Communicating

You should not only communicate clearly what you want done, you should also encourage people to communicate with one another.

Avoid situations in which people can say: 'Why didn't someone tell me about this? If they had, I could have told them how to get out of the difficulty.' Nobody should be allowed to resort to the old excuse that 'no one tells me anything'. It is up to people to find out what they need to know and not wait to be told.

Controlling

If you use the processes described above, and they work, theoretically you will not have to worry any more about coordination.

But, of course, life is not like that. You must monitor actions and results, spot problems and take swift corrective action when necessary. Coordination doesn't just happen. It has to be worked at – but avoid getting too involved. Allow people as much freedom as possible to develop horizontal relationships. These can facilitate coordination far more effectively than rigid and authoritarian control from above.

CASE STUDY

There is no one right way of coordinating a number of activities.

It all depends on the nature of the activities and the circumstances in which they are carried out: for example, the present organization structure, the existence of coordinating committees and the facility with which communication can take place between those involved. Ultimately, good coordination depends upon the will of everyone concerned – to coordinate or be coordinated. Formal devices such as committees will not necessarily do the trick.

An example of good coordination took place in a company that was developing a new product in a new market. Neither the product nor the market fitted conveniently into the existing divisional structure and it was therefore decided to appoint one man as project manager to get the product launched. He would have a staff of two: a brand manager and a secretary. The work of development, production, marketing, selling and customer servicing would be carried out by the relevant departments in various divisions of the company.

The project manager had the status and authority to get things done by each department. The board was right behind the project and had allocated the priorities and resources required. But the different activities had to be coordinated and only the project manager could do it.

The easy way out would have been to set up a massive coordinating committee and leave it at that. This would have failed. Projects of this complexity cannot be coordinated just by creating a committee.

The project manager developed a different approach that proved to be highly successful. His first objective was to make everyone concerned enthusiastic about the project. He wanted them to believe in its importance so that they would be committed to working closely with the other departments involved.

His next step was to hold separate discussions with departmental heads so that they completely understood the programme of work required in each area. With the help of a project planner he then drew up a chart showing the key events and activities, the relationships between them, and the sequence in which they needed to take place in order to complete the project. This chart was distributed to all the departmental heads and supplemented by an explanatory brief on the work required at each stage of the programme. Only then did he call a meeting to iron out difficulties and to ensure that everyone knew what had to be done and when.

He set up a system of progress reports and held progress meetings with departmental heads. But these were only held as necessary and he did not rely upon them to achieve coordination. He depended much more on personal contacts with individual managers, reviewing problems, noting where adjustments to the programme were needed, and stimulating the managers to even greater efforts when required. It was time consuming, but it kept him closely in touch so that he could anticipate any likely delays, setbacks or failures in communication, and be in a position to take action. He used the chart as his main instrument for checking that the critical events took place as planned.

The successful coordination and completion of the project were not achieved by one method but by the judicious use of a combination of techniques relevant to the situation: motivating, team building, planning, integrating, monitoring and controlling.

How to delegate 13

Delegation is the process of allocating work for members of your team to do. You can't do everything yourself, so you have to delegate. At first sight delegation looks simple: just tell people what you want them to do and then let them do it. But there is more to it than that.

It may be that you would wish to delegate everything except what an individual team member is not able to do. But you cannot then withdraw. You have arranged for someone else to do the job, but you have not passed on the responsibility for it. You are always accountable to your boss for what anyone who works for you does.

Hence, as is often said, you can't delegate responsibility.

Delegation is difficult. It is perhaps the hardest task for managers. The problem is achieving the right balance between delegating too much or too little and between over- or under-supervision. When you give people a job to do you have to make sure that it is done. And you have to do that without breathing down their necks, wasting your time and theirs, and getting in the way. There must be trust as well as guidance and supervision.

Advantages of delegation

1 It relieves you of routine and less critical tasks, and it frees you for more important work.

2 It extends your capacity to manage.

3 It reduces delay in decision-making – as long as authority is delegated close to the point of action.

4 It allows decisions to be taken at the level where the details are known.

5 It develops the abilities and confidence of staff.

The process of delegation

Delegation is a process that can follow a sequence from total control (no freedom of action for the individual to whom work has been allocated) to full devolution (the individual is completely empowered to carry out the work), as illustrated in Figure 13.1.

Figure 13.1   The sequence of delegation

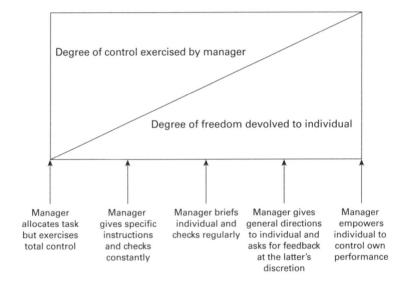

Degree of control exercised by manager

Degree of freedom devolved to individual

| Manager allocates task but exercises total control | Manager gives specific instructions and checks constantly | Manager briefs individual and checks regularly | Manager gives general directions to individual and asks for feedback at the latter's discretion | Manager empowers individual to control own performance |

When to delegate

You should delegate when:

- you have more work than you can effectively carry out yourself;
- you cannot allocate sufficient time to your priority tasks;

- you want to develop your subordinate;
- the job can be done adequately by your subordinate.

How to delegate

When you delegate you have to decide:

- what to delegate;
- to whom you delegate – choosing who does the work;
- how to inform or brief the individual – giving out the work;
- how you will guide and develop the individual;
- how you will monitor the individual's performance.

What to delegate

You delegate tasks that you don't need to do yourself. You are not just ridding yourself of the difficult, tedious or unrewarding tasks. Neither are you trying to win for yourself an easier life. Delegation will, in fact, make your life more difficult, but also more rewarding.

Clearly, you delegate routine and repetitive tasks that you cannot reasonably be expected to do yourself – as long as you use the time you have won productively.

You also delegate specialist tasks to those who have the skills and know-how to do them. You cannot do it all yourself. Nor can you be expected to know it all yourself. You have to know how to select and use expertise. There will be no problem as long as you make it clear what you want from the experts and ask them to present it to you in a usable way. As a manager, you must know what specialists can do for you and you should be knowledgeable enough about the subject to understand whether or not what they produce is worth having.

Choosing who does the work

Ideally, the person you choose to do the work should have the knowledge, skills, motivation and time needed to get it done to your complete satisfaction. Frequently, however, you will have to use someone who has less than ideal experience, knowledge or skills. In these cases, you should try to select an individual who has intelligence, natural aptitude and, above all, willingness to learn how to do the job with help and guidance. This is how people develop, and the development of your staff should be your conscious aim whenever you delegate.

You are looking for someone you can trust. You don't want to over-supervise, so you have to believe that the person you select will get on with it and have the sense to come to you when stuck or before making a bad mistake.

How do you know whom you can trust? The best way is to try people out first on smaller and less important tasks, increasingly giving them more scope so that they learn how far they can go and you can observe how they do it. If they get on well, their sense of responsibility and powers of judgement will increase and improve and you will be able to trust them with more demanding and responsible tasks.

Giving out the work

When you delegate you should ensure that individuals understand:

- why the work needs to be done;
- what they are expected to do;
- the date by which they are expected to do it;
- the authority they have to make decisions;
- the problems they must refer back;
- the progress or completion reports they should submit;
- how you propose to guide and monitor them;
- the resources and help they will have to complete the work.

People may need guidance on how the work should be done. The extent to which you spell it out will clearly depend on how much they already know about how to do the work. You don't want to give directions in such laborious detail that you run the risk of stifling initiative. As long as you are sure they will do the job without breaking the law, exceeding the budget, embarrassing you or seriously upsetting people, let them get on with it. Follow Robert Heller's[1] golden rule: 'If you can't do something yourself, find someone who can – and then let him do it in his own sweet way.'

You can make a distinction between hard and soft delegation

Hard delegation takes place when you tell someone exactly what to do, how to do it and when you want the results. You spell it out, confirm it in writing and make a note in your diary of the date when you expect the job to be completed. And then you follow up regularly.

Soft delegation takes place when you agree generally what has to be achieved and leave the individual to get on with it. You should still agree limits of authority, define the decisions to be referred to you, say what exception reports you want (see Chapter 11), and indicate when and how you will review progress. Then you sit back until the results are due and observe from afar, only coming closer for periodical progress meetings, or when the exception report suggests that something needs looking into, or when a problem or decision is referred to you.

You should always delegate by the results you expect. Even if you do not need to specify exactly how the results should be achieved, it is a good idea when delegating a problem to ask people how they propose to solve it. You then have the opportunity to provide guidance at the outset; guidance at a later stage may be seen as interference.

Guidance and development

Delegation not only helps you to get your work done; it can be used to improve the individual's performance and therefore your trust in their ability to carry out more responsible work. Instruction, training and development are part of the process of delegation.

Monitoring performance

At first you may have to monitor the individual's performance carefully, but the sooner you can relax and watch progress informally the better.

You will have set target dates, and you should keep a reminder of these in your diary so that you can ensure they are achieved. Don't allow anyone to become careless about meeting deadlines.

Without being oppressive, you should ensure that progress reports are made when required and that you discuss deviations from the original plan in good time. You will have clearly indicated to individuals the extent of their authority to act without further reference to you. They must therefore expect to be reprimanded if on any occasion they exceed their brief or fail to keep you informed. You don't want any surprises and individuals must understand that you will not tolerate being kept in the dark.

Try to restrain yourself from undue interference in the way the work is being done. It is, after all, the results that count. Of course, you must step in if there is any danger of things going off the rails. The Nelson touch is all right if your subordinate is a Nelson, but how many Nelsons have you got? Rash decisions, over-expenditure and ignoring defined and reasonable constraints and rules must be prevented.

There is a delicate balance to be achieved between hedging people around with restrictions that may appear petty and allowing them licence to do what they like. You must use your knowledge of your people and the circumstances to decide where the balance should be struck. The best delegators are those who have a comprehensive understanding of the strengths and weaknesses of their staff and the situation in which they are working.

Above all, avoid 'river banking'. This happens when a boss gives someone a task that is more or less impossible to do. As the individual is 'going down' for the third time the boss is observed in a remote and safe position on the river bank saying: 'It's easy really, all you need to do is to try a bit harder.'

The thoughts of some successful delegators

John H Johnson, editor and publisher of Johnson Publishing Company, chief executive officer of Supreme Life Insurance Company and a board member of many large US corporations, said of his delegation techniques: 'I want to be big and I want to be bigger and I can't do it all by myself. So I try to do only those things that I can't get anyone else to do.'

Franklin D Roosevelt used a particularly ruthless technique based on competition when he requested his aides to find some information. One of them told the story as follows:

> He would call you in, and he'd ask you to get the story on some complicated business and you'd come back after a couple of days of hard labour and present the juicy morsel you'd uncovered under a stone somewhere and then you'd find out he knew all about it, along with something else you didn't know. Where he got this information from he wouldn't mention, usually, but after he had done this to you once or twice you got damn careful about your information.

Robert Townsend's approach to delegation when he was chairman of Avis was to emphasize the need to delegate 'as many important matters as you can because that creates a climate in which people grow'.

When he started, the head of a supermarket chain told his division managers: 'I don't know anything about the grocery business but you fellows do. From now on, you're running your division as if it were your own business. You don't take orders from anyone but me and I'm not going to give you orders. I'm going to hold you responsible.'

Franklin Moore related the following example of strong delegation: Ralf Cordiner, the head of General Electric in the United States for 10 years, had a vice president who wanted to see him urgently about a problem. The vice president explained his problem, and the choices he thought he had. 'Now, Mr Cordiner,' he said, 'what should I do?' 'Do?' Cordiner answered, 'You'd damn well better get on an airplane and get back to your office and decide. And if you can't decide we'd better get someone who can.'

Peter Drucker,[2] writing about responsibility, referred to a news-paper interview with a young American infantry captain in the Vietnam jungle. The reporter asked: 'How in this confused situation can you retain command?' The captain replied:

> Around here, I am the only guy who is responsible. If these men don't know what to do when they run into an enemy in the jungle, I'm too far away to tell them. My job is to make sure they know. What they do depends on the situation that only they can judge. The responsibility is always mine, but the decision lies with whoever is on the spot.

CASE STUDY

A group of researchers studying how managers delegate found that the following was happening in one of the companies they were studying:

> *In the situations in which the men we were interviewing found themselves, the boss was usually a hurried, and sometimes a harried, man. He gave out broad, briefly stated assignments, expecting his subordinates to make sense out of them. He also expected them to decide what information they needed, to obtain that information and then to go ahead and carry out their assignments. In the case of repetitive tasks, the typical boss assumed that after a few trials his subordinates would know for themselves when a job needed doing.*

> *Frequently the boss wasn't sure himself about which issues needed attention in his department. And although he knew what eventually had to be accomplished, often he had less idea than his subordinates about the approaches to take. It wasn't unusual, therefore, for the boss to be vague or even impatient when approached with questions about the job while it was going on.*

Usually he was much more assertive in describing what he wanted after a job was done than while it was in progress.

The production director came out of the board of directors' meeting where he had been roundly criticized for not getting the most out of his organization. He immediately called a meeting of his subordinates and told them: 'I don't intend to subject myself to such humiliation again. You men are paid to do your jobs; it's not up to me to do them for you. I don't know how you spend your time and I don't intend to try to find out. You know your responsibilities, and these figures bear out that you haven't discharged them properly. If the next report doesn't show a marked improvement, there will be some new faces around here.'

Endnotes

1 Heller, R (1972) *The Naked Manager*, Barrie & Jenkins, London
2 Drucker, P (1967) *The Effective Executive*, Heinemann, London

How to make things happen

14

Making things happen, getting things done, achieving results – this is what management is all about.

It can be said that there are three sorts of managers: those who make things happen, those who watch things happening, and those who don't know what is happening. Before finding out how to get into the first category, there are three questions to answer:

1 Is getting things done simply a matter of personality – characteristics like drive, decisiveness, leadership, ambition – which some people have and others haven't?

2 And if you haven't got the drive, decisiveness and so forth that it takes, is there anything you can do about it?

3 To what extent is an ability to make things happen a matter of using techniques that can be learnt and developed?

Personality is important. Unless you have willpower and drive, nothing will get done. But remember that your personality is a function of both nature and nurture. You are born with certain characteristics. Upbringing, education, training and, above all, experience, develop you into the person you are.

We may not be able to change our personality, which, according to Freud, is formed in the first few years of life. But we can develop and adapt it by consciously learning from our own experience and by observing and analysing other people's behaviour.

Techniques for achieving results, such as planning, organizing, delegating, communicating, motivating and controlling, can be learnt. These are dealt with in this book. But these techniques are only as effective as the person who uses them. They must be applied in the right way and in the right circumstances. And you still have to use your experience to select the right technique and your personality to make it work.

To become a person who makes things happen, you therefore have to develop skills and capacities by a process of understanding, observation, analysis and learning.

The four actions you should take are:

- understand what makes achievers tick – the personality characteristics they display in getting things done;

- observe what achievers do – how they operate, what techniques they use;

- analyse your own behaviour (behaviour, not personality), compare it with that of high achievers, and think how to improve your effectiveness;

- learn as much as you can about the management techniques available.

What makes achievers tick?

David McClelland[1] of Harvard University carried out extensive research into what motivates managers. He interviewed, observed and analysed numbers of managers at their place of work and identified three needs that he believed were key factors in motivating managers. These are:

1 the need for achievement;

2 the need for power (having control and influence over people);

3 the need for affiliation (to be accepted by others).

All effective managers have these needs to a certain degree, but by far the most important one is achievement.

Achievement is what counts and achievers, according to McClelland, have these characteristics:

- They set themselves realistic but achievable goals with some 'stretch' built in.

- They prefer situations that they themselves can influence rather than those on which chance has a large influence.
- They are more concerned with knowing they have done well than with the rewards that success brings.
- They get their rewards from their accomplishment rather than from money or praise. This does not mean that high achievers reject money, which does in fact motivate them as long as it is seen as a realistic measure of performance.
- High achievers are most effective in situations where they are allowed to get ahead by their own efforts.

What do achievers do?

High achievers do some, if not all, of the following:

- They define to themselves precisely what they want to do.
- They set demanding but not unattainable timescales in which to do it.
- They convey clearly what they want done and by when.
- They are prepared to discuss how things should be done and will listen to and take advice. But once the course of action has been agreed they stick to it unless events dictate a change of direction.
- They are single-minded about getting where they want to go, showing perseverance and determination in the face of adversity.
- They demand high performance from themselves and are somewhat callous in expecting equally high performance from everyone else.
- They work hard and work well under pressure; in fact, it brings out the best in them.
- They tend to be dissatisfied with the status quo.
- They are never completely satisfied with their own performance and continually question themselves.
- They will take calculated risks.

- They snap out of setbacks without being personally shattered and quickly regroup their forces and their ideas.

- They are enthusiastic about the task and convey their enthusiasm to others.

- They are decisive in the sense that they are able quickly to sum up situations, define alternative courses of action, determine the preferred course, and convey to their subordinates what needs to be done.

- They continually monitor their own and their subordinates' performance so that any deviation can be corrected in good time.

How to analyse your own behaviour

It is no good trying to analyse your own behaviour unless you have criteria against which you can measure your performance. You have to set standards for yourself, and if you don't meet them, ask yourself why. The answer should tell you what to do next time.

The basic questions you should ask yourself are:

1 What did I set out to do?

2 Did I get it done?

3 If I did, why and how did I succeed?

4 If not, why not?

The aim is to make effective use of your experience.

Use the list of what high achievers do to check your own behaviour and actions. If your performance has not been up to scratch under any of these headings, ask yourself specifically what went wrong and decide how you are going to overcome this difficulty next time. This is not always easy. It is hard to admit to yourself, for example, that you have not been sufficiently enthusiastic. It may be even harder to decide what to do about it. You don't want to enthuse all over the place, indiscriminately. But you can consider whether there are better ways of displaying and conveying your enthusiasm to others in order to carry them with you.

Learning

There are a number of management skills and techniques that you need to know about. These techniques are discussed in other chapters in this book. The ones you should be particularly interested in are:

- communicating;
- controlling;
- coordinating;
- decision-making;
- delegating;
- leadership;
- motivating;
- planning and prioritizing;
- project management.

Conclusion

This process of observation, analysis and learning will help you to become an achiever. But remember, achieving results is ultimately about making promises – to others and to yourself – and keeping them. Robert Townsend[2] in his book *Up the Organization*, has some excellent advice: 'Promises: keep. If asked when you can deliver something, ask for time to think. Build in a margin of safety. Name a date. Then deliver it earlier than you promised.'

Endnotes

1 McClelland, D (1975) *Power: The inner experience*, Irvington, New York

2 Townsend, R (1970) *Up the Organization*, Michael Joseph, London

How to manage your boss 15

If you want to achieve results, innovate and get on, you have to learn how to manage your boss. The word 'manage' is defined in the *Oxford English Dictionary* as:

- to conduct affairs;
- to control; cause to submit to one's rule;
- to bring (a person) to consent to one's wishes by artifice, flattery, or judicious suggestion of motives;
- to operate upon, manipulate for a purpose;
- to bring to pass by contrivance;
- to succeed in accomplishing;
- to deal with or treat carefully.

Although such concepts as artifice, flattery and manipulation should not normally play any part, all these definitions provide clues to the various aspects of managing one's boss.

If you really believe that something needs to be done and you cannot do it without the consent of your boss, you have to work out how you are going to manage him or her. And it is worth careful and continuous thought. It is too easy to neglect this essential part of the art of management.

To manage your boss, you need to know how to:

1 get agreement from him or her on what you want to do;
2 deal with him or her over problems;
3 impress him or her, so that they are more likely to accept your proposals and to place their trust in you.

Getting agreement

Getting agreement from bosses is in many ways like getting agreement from anyone else. You need to be good at case presentation and at persuasion. More specifically you need to do the following things:

- Find out what they expect.

- Learn about their likes and dislikes, their quirks and their prejudices.

- Establish how they like things presented to them. Do they like long, carefully worked out, written reports? Or do they prefer a succinct proposal on one side of one sheet of paper? Perhaps they are more likely to be persuaded if they are introduced gradually to a proposal – a softening-up process, as it were. It is often advisable to test the water before plunging straight in. Some people prefer to start by talking all the way around a problem before getting down to its essential elements. They don't like surprises.

- Get to know how they like things done – by observation and by asking other people. If something goes wrong, choose the right moment and ask their advice on how to do it better next time (most people love being asked for their advice).

- Find out the right time to approach them. Some people are at their best first thing. Others take time to warm up. It is obviously inadvisable to spring surprises on someone at the end of a long, hard day. Check on their mood in advance. PAs can help, and it is always worthwhile having these people on your side. PAs can be good friends but bad enemies.

- Work out the best circumstances in which to tackle them: alone in the office, or over lunch, or driving at speed along a motorway (there is a lot to be said for a captive audience). Getting away from the office may be an advantage: there will be no interruptions and your boss is less likely to call in the henchman, so you will not have to persuade two people at once (picking them off one at a time is much more likely to be successful). Beware of the 'abominable no-man'. Most organizations have at least one – often the head of finance. They no doubt perform a useful role, but keep them out of your way if you can.

- Decide whether you want support. You may be able to make a better case on a one-to-one basis. There is a lot to be said for standing firmly on your own two feet.

- Don't go in for open confrontation if you cannot get your own way at first. Get agreement on the points your boss is prepared to agree, and then turn to the problem areas. Impress upon your boss that you want the two of you to cover every possible angle. Emphasize joint responsibility.

- Leave them an escape route – a way open to consent without their having to climb down. Don't beat them into the ground – you might win this one but what about the next time?

- Don't overwhelm them with your ideas. Don't expect to achieve everything at once. Tackle one important thing at a time. Keep it simple. If you come up against a strong objection, don't fight it for too long. Survive to fight another day. This does not mean that you should not argue your case strongly, but that you should avoid giving the impression of being pigheaded.

- Keep in reserve alternative proposals or modifications to your original idea to use if you are getting nowhere.

- If your boss comes up with a better idea than yours, recognize and accept it. Everybody likes recognition. There is no need to flatter them. You are only reacting to them the way you would like them to react to you.

- If you can't convince your boss first time, remember who is the boss. Bosses make the ultimate decisions. If they say 'That's the way it's going to be', you may have to accept it. In the end your boss could say to you: 'We're in a two-horse race and only one can win, and that's going to be me.' But you don't have to give up completely. Watch for any signs that your boss might be prepared to change his or her mind – given time and a revision to your argument or proposal.

- Don't nag. If you press too hard they will become stubborn and begin to think you are challenging their authority and position. Retire in good order and re-open your campaign at the right moment.

Dealing with problems

Things are going wrong. You've made a mistake. You need your boss's help in sorting out a problem. How do you tackle him or her? You should adopt the following approach:

- Keep your boss informed. Never let them be taken by surprise. Prepare them in advance for the bad news. If 'troubles come not in single spies but in battalions', don't let them have it all at once. Let them down as gently as possible. Don't use the 'first the good news, then the bad news' line too crudely, but don't be too gloomy. Give them hope.

- If something has gone wrong, explain what has happened, why it has happened (no excuses) and what you would like to do about it. Don't dump the problem in their lap in a 'take it or leave it' spirit.

- Emphasize that you are seeking their views on what you propose, as well as their agreement.

- If you think your boss is to blame, never say, 'I told you so.' If you do, you will make an enemy for life.

- If you admit responsibility, try to stop your boss keeping on at you. Steer him or her away from recriminations into a positive attitude on what you can jointly do to solve the problem.

Impressing your boss

Your purpose as a manager is not solely to impress the bosses. Nor is it to make them like you. But you will get more done and get on better if you impress them. And why make an enemy of your boss when you can have him or her as a friend?

Your boss needs to trust you, to rely upon you and to believe in your capacity to come up with good ideas and to make things happen. He or she doesn't want to wet-nurse you or to spend time correcting your mistakes or covering up.

To succeed in impressing your boss without really trying – it's fatal to push too much – you should:

- Always be frank and open. Admit mistakes. Never lie or even shade the truth. If there is the faintest suspicion that you are not perfectly straightforward, your boss will never trust you again.

- Aim to help your boss to be right. This does not mean being subservient or time-serving. Recognize, however, that you exist to give him or her support – in the right direction.

- Respond fast to requests on a can do/will do basis.

- Don't trouble him or her unnecessarily with your problems.

- Provide him or her with protection where required. Loyalty is an old-fashioned virtue, but you owe it to your boss. If you cannot be loyal then you should get out from under as quick as you can.

Completed staff work

Always provide your boss with what the army calls 'completed staff work'. This means that if you are asked to do something you should do it thoroughly. Come up with solutions, not problems. Test your ideas in draft form if you like, but, having done so, present a complete proposal with whatever supporting arguments or evidence you need. Avoid half-baked suggestions. Your boss wants answers, not questions. When you have finished your report and studied your conclusions and recommendations, ask yourself the question: 'If I were my boss would I stake my reputation on this piece of work and put my name to it?' If the answer is 'No', tear up your report and do it again. It's not completed staff work.

How to manage change 16

Change is the only constant process that exists in organizations. An effective organization is one that takes deliberate steps to manage change smoothly. It will not always succeed – change can be a traumatic process – but at least it will try, and attempts to manage change will have the minimum objective of mitigating its effects on the organization and its employees.

The approach to the management of change will recognize that the key to success lies not only in a transformational leader supported by powerful change mechanisms, but also in understanding that change is implemented by people and that it is their behaviour and support that count. The most important aim of change management is to achieve commitment to change.

Successful change management requires an understanding of:

- the main types of change;
- how change affects individuals;
- the process of change;
- how to build commitment to change.

Types of change

There are two main types of change: strategic and operational.

Strategic change

Strategic change is concerned with broad, long-term and organization-wide issues. It is about moving to a future state that has been defined generally in terms of strategic vision and scope. It will cover the purpose and mission of the organization, its corporate philosophy on such matters as growth, quality, innovation and values concerning people, the customer needs served and the technologies employed. This overall definition leads to specifications of competitive positioning and strategic goals for achieving and maintaining competitive advantage and for product market development. These goals are supported by policies concerning marketing, sales, manufacturing, product and process development, finance and human resource management.

Strategic change takes place within the context of the external competitive, economic and social environment, and the organization's internal resources, capabilities, culture, structure and systems. Its successful implementation requires thorough analysis and understanding of these factors in the formulation and planning stages.

Operational change

Operational change relates to new systems, procedures, structures or technology that will have an immediate effect on working arrangements within a part of the organization. But the impact of such changes on people can be more significant than broader strategic change and they have to be handled just as carefully.

How people change

The ways in which people change are best explained by reference to the assumptions developed by Bandura[1] that people make conscious choices about their behaviour and the information people use to make their choices comes from their environment. Their choices are based upon:

- the things that are important to them;
- the views they have about their own abilities to behave in certain ways;
- the consequences they think will accrue from whatever behaviour they decide to engage in.

This implies that:

1 The tighter the link between a particular behaviour and a particular outcome, the more likely it is that we will engage in that behaviour.

2 The more desirable the outcome, the more likely it is that we will engage in behaviour that we believe will lead to it.

3 The more confident we are that we can actually assume a new behaviour, the more likely we are to try it.

To change people's behaviour, therefore, we have first to change the environment within which they work; second, to convince them that the new behaviour is something they can accomplish (training is important); and third, to persuade them that it will lead to an outcome that they will value. None of these steps is easy. To achieve them, it helps to know more about the process of change.

The process of change

Change, as Rosabeth Moss Kanter[2] puts it, is the process of analysing 'the past to elicit the present actions required for the future'. It involves moving from a present state, through a transitional state, to a future desired state.

The process starts with an awareness of the need for change. An analysis of the present state and the factors that have created it leads to a diagnosis of the distinctive characteristics of the situation and an indication of the direction in which action needs to be taken. Possible courses of action can then be identified and evaluated and a choice made of the preferred action.

It is then necessary to decide how to get from here to there. Managing the change process in this transitional state is a critical phase in the change process. It is here that the problems of introducing change emerge and have to be managed. These problems can include resistance to change, low stability, high levels of stress, misdirected energy, conflict and loss of momentum. Hence the need to do everything possible to anticipate reactions and likely impediments to the introduction of change.

The installation stage can also be painful. When planning change, there is a tendency for people to think that it will be an entirely logical and linear process of going from A to B. It is not like that at all. As described by Pettigrew and Whipp,[3] the implementation of change is an 'iterative, cumulative and reformulation-in-use process'.

The approach to change management

Michael Beer and his colleagues suggested in a seminal *Harvard Business Review* article, 'Why change programs don't produce change',[3] that most such programmes are guided by a theory of change that is fundamentally flawed. This theory states that changes in attitude lead to changes in behaviour. 'According to this model, change is like a conversion experience. Once people "get religion", changes in their behaviour will surely follow.'

They believe that this theory gets the change process exactly backwards:

> In fact, individual behaviour is powerfully shaped by the organizational roles people play. The most effective way to change behaviour, therefore, is to put people into a new organizational context, which imposes new roles, responsibilities and relationships on them. This creates a situation that in a sense 'forces' new attitudes and behaviour on people.

They prescribe six steps to effective change that concentrate on what they call 'task alignment' – reorganizing employees' roles, responsibilities and relationships to solve specific business problems in small units where goals and tasks can be clearly defined.

The aim of following the overlapping steps is to build a self-reinforcing cycle of commitment, coordination and competence. The steps are:

- mobilize commitment to change through the joint analysis of problems;
- develop a shared vision of how to organize and manage to achieve goals such as competitiveness;

- foster consensus for the new vision, competence to enact it, and cohesion to move it along;
- spread revitalization to all departments without pushing it from the top – don't force the issue, let each department find its own way to the new organization;
- institutionalize revitalization through formal policies, systems and structures;
- monitor and adjust strategies in response to problems in the revitalization process.

The approach suggested by Michael Beer and his colleagues is fundamental to the effective management of change. It can, however, be associated with a number of other guidelines as set out below.

Guidelines on how to facilitate change have been produced by General Electric. These are to ensure that:

- employees see the reason for change;
- employees understand why change is important and see how it will help them and the business in the long and short term;
- the people who need to be committed to the change to make it happen are recognized;
- a coalition of support is built for the change;
- the support of key individuals in the organization is enlisted;
- the link between the change and other HR systems such as staffing, training, appraisal, rewards, structure and communication is understood;
- the systems implications of the change are recognized;
- a means of measuring the success of the change is identified;
- plans are made to monitor progress in the implementation of change;
- the first steps in getting change started are recognized;
- plans are made to keep attention focused on the change;
- the likely need to adapt the change over time is recognized and plans can readily be made and implemented for such adaptations.

Guidelines for change management

- The achievement of sustainable change requires strong commitment and visionary leadership from the top.

- Understanding is necessary of the culture of the organization and the levers for change most likely to be effective therein.

- Those concerned with managing change at all levels should have the temperament and leadership skills appropriate to the circumstances of the organization and its change strategies.

- It is important to build a working environment that is conducive to change. This means developing the firm as a 'learning organization'.

- Although there may be an overall strategy for change, it is best tackled incrementally (except in crisis conditions). The change programme should be broken down into actionable segments for which people can be held accountable.

- The reward system should encourage innovation and recognize success in achieving change.

- Change implies streams of activity across time and 'may require the enduring of abortive efforts or the build-up of slow incremental phases of adjustment which then allow short bursts of incremental action to take place' – Pettigrew and Whipp.[4]

- Change will always involve failure as well as success. The failures must be expected and learned from.

- Hard evidence and data on the need for change are the most powerful tools for its achievement, but establishing the need for change is easier than deciding how to satisfy it.

- It is easier to change behaviour by changing processes, structures and systems than to change attitudes or the corporate culture.

- There are always people in organizations who welcome the challenges and opportunities that change can provide. They are the ones to be chosen as change agents.

- Resistance to change is inevitable if the individuals concerned feel that they are going to be worse off – implicitly or explicitly. The inept management of change will produce that reaction.

- In an age of global competition, technological innovation, turbulence, discontinuity, even chaos, change is inevitable and necessary. The organization must do all it can to explain why change is essential and how it will affect everyone. Moreover, every effort must be made to protect the interests of those affected by change.

Gaining commitment to change

These guidelines point in one direction: having decided why changes are necessary, what the goals are and how they are to be achieved, the most important task is to gain the commitment of all concerned to the proposed change.

A strategy for gaining commitment to change should cover the following phases:

1 *Preparation* – in this phase, the person or persons likely to be affected by the proposed change are contacted in order to be made aware of it.

2 *Acceptance* – in the second phase, information is provided on the purpose of the change, how it is proposed to implement it and what effect it will have on those concerned. The aim is to achieve understanding of what the change means and to obtain a positive reaction. This is more likely if:

- the change is perceived to be consistent with the mission and values of the organization;

- the change is not thought to be threatening;

- the change seems likely to meet the needs of those concerned;

- there is a compelling and fully understood reason for change;

- those concerned are involved in planning and implementing the change programme on the principle that people support what they help to create;

- it is understood that steps will be taken to mitigate any detrimental effects of the change.

It may be difficult, even impossible to meet these requirements. That is why the problems of gaining commitment to change should not be underestimated.

During this phase, the extent to which reactions are positive or negative can be noted and action taken accordingly. It is at this stage that original plans may have to be modified to cater for legitimate reservations or second thoughts.

3 *Commitment* – during the third phase, the change is implemented and becomes operational. The change process and people's reaction to it need to be monitored. There will inevitably be delays, setbacks, unforeseen problems and negative reactions from those faced with the reality of change. A response to these reactions is essential so that valid criticisms can be acted upon or reasons given as to why the change should proceed as planned.

Following implementation, the aim is to have the change adopted, as its worth becomes evident with use. The decision is made at this stage whether to continue with the change or to modify or even abort it. Account should again be taken of the views of those involved.

Finally, and after further modifications as required, the change is institutionalized and becomes an inherent part of the organization's culture and operations.

Endnotes

1 Bandura, A (1986) *Social Boundaries of Thought and Action*, Prentice-Hall, Englewood Cliffs, NJ

2 Kanter, R M (1984) *The Change Masters*, Allen & Unwin, London

3 Beer, M, Eisenstat, R and Specter, B (1990) Why change programs don't produce change, *Harvard Business Review*, November–December

4 Pettigrew, A and Whipp, R (1991) *Managing Change for Competitive Success*, Blackwell, Oxford

How to manage conflict 17

Conflict is inevitable in organizations because the objectives, values and needs of groups and individuals do not always coincide. Conflict may be a sign of a healthy organization. Bland agreement on everything would be unnatural and enervating. There should be clashes of ideas about tasks and projects, and disagreements should not be suppressed. They should come out into the open because that is the only way to ensure that the issues are explored and conflicts are resolved.

There is such a thing as creative conflict – new or modified ideas, insights, approaches and solutions can be generated by a joint re-examination of the different points of view as long as this is based on an objective and rational exchange of information and ideas. But conflict becomes counterproductive when it is based on personality clashes, or when it is treated as an unseemly mess to be hurriedly cleared away, rather than as a problem to be worked through.

Conflict resolution can be concerned with conflict between groups or between individuals.

Handling inter-group conflict

There are three principal ways of resolving inter-group conflict: peaceful coexistence, compromise and problem-solving.

Peaceful coexistence

The aim here is to smooth out differences and emphasize the common ground. People are encouraged to learn to live together;

there is a good deal of information, contact and exchange of views, and individuals move freely between groups (for example, between headquarters and the field, or between sales and manufacturing).

This is a pleasant ideal, but it may not be practicable in many situations. There is much evidence that conflict is not necessarily resolved by bringing people together. Improved communications and techniques such as briefing groups may appear to be good ideas but are useless if management has nothing to say that people want to hear. There is also the danger that the real issues, submerged for the moment in an atmosphere of superficial bonhomie, will surface again later.

Compromise

The issue is resolved by negotiation or bargaining and neither party wins or loses. This concept of splitting the difference is essentially pessimistic. The hallmark of this approach is that there is no 'right' or 'best' answer. Agreements only accommodate differences. Real issues are not likely to be solved.

Problem-solving

An attempt is made to find a genuine solution to the problem rather than just accommodating different points of view. This is where the apparent paradox of 'creative conflict' comes in. Conflict situations can be used to advantage to create better solutions.

If solutions are to be developed by problem-solving, they have to be generated by those who share the responsibility for seeing that the solutions work. The sequence of actions is: first, those concerned work to define the problem and agree on the objectives to be attained in reaching a solution; second, the group develops alternative solutions and debates their merits; third, agreement is reached on the preferred course of action and how it should be implemented.

Handling conflict between individuals

Handling interpersonal conflict can be even more difficult than resolving conflicts between groups. Whether the conflict is openly hostile or subtly covert, strong personal feelings may be involved. Yet, as James Ware and Louis Barnes[1] say:

> The ability to productively manage such conflict is critical to managerial success. Interpersonal differences often become sharpest when the organizational stakes seem to be high, but almost all organizations include their share of small issues blown into major conflicts. The manager's problem is to build on human differences of opinion while not letting them jeopardize overall performance, satisfaction and growth.

Ware and Barnes go on to say that interpersonal conflict, like intergroup conflict, is an organizational reality that is neither good nor bad. It can be destructive, but it can also play a productive role. 'Problems usually arise when potential conflict is artificially suppressed, or when it escalates beyond the control of the adversaries or third-party intermediaries.'

The reaction to interpersonal conflict may be the withdrawal of either party, leaving the other one to hold the field. This is the classic win–lose situation. The problem has been resolved by force, but this may not be the best solution if it represents one person's point of view that has ignored counter-arguments, and has, in fact, steamrollered over them. The winner may be triumphant but the loser will be aggrieved and either demotivated or resolved to fight again another day. There will have been a lull in, but not an end to, the conflict.

Another approach is to smooth over differences and pretend that the conflict does not exist, although no attempt has been made to tackle the root causes. Again, this is an unsatisfactory approach. The issue is likely to re-emerge and the battle will recommence.

Yet another approach is bargaining to reach a compromise.

This means that both sides are prepared to lose as well as win some points and the aim is to reach a solution acceptable to both sides. Bargaining, however, involves all sorts of tactical and often counterproductive games, and the parties are often more anxious to seek acceptable compromises than to achieve sound solutions.

Ware and Barnes identify two other approaches to managing interpersonal conflict: controlling, and constructive confrontation.

Controlling conflict

Controlling conflict can involve preventing interaction, or structuring the forms of interaction or reducing or changing external pressures.

Preventing interaction is a strategy for use when emotions are high. Conflict is controlled by keeping the conflicting parties apart in the hope that, although the differences still exist, the people involved will have time to cool down and consider more constructive approaches. But this may only be a temporary expedient and the eventual confrontation could be even more explosive.

Structuring the forms of interaction is a strategy that can be used when it is not possible to separate the parties. In these cases, ground rules can be developed to deal with the conflict concerning such behaviours as communicating information or dealing with specific issues. However, this may also be a temporary strategy if the strong underlying feelings are only suppressed rather than resolved.

Personal counselling is an approach that does not address the conflict itself but focuses on how the two people are reacting. Personal counselling gives people a chance to release pent-up tensions and may encourage them to think about new ways of resolving the conflict. But it does not address the essential nature of the conflict, which is the relationship between two people.

Thus, constructive confrontation offers the best hope of a long-term solution.

Constructive confrontation

Constructive confrontation is a method of bringing the individuals in conflict together, ideally with a third party whose function is to help build an exploratory and cooperative climate.

Constructive confrontation aims to get the parties involved to understand and explore each other's perceptions and feelings. It is a process of developing mutual understanding to produce a win–win situation. The issues will be confronted but on the basis of a joint analysis, with the help of the third party, of facts relating to the situation and the actual behaviour of those involved. Feelings will be expressed but they will be analysed by reference to specific events and behaviours rather than inferences or speculations about motives.

Third parties have a key role in this process, and it is not an easy one. They have to get agreement to the ground rules for discussions aimed at bringing out the facts and minimizing hostile behaviour. They must monitor the ways in which negative feelings are expressed and encourage the parties to produce new definitions of the problem and its cause or causes and new motives to reach a common solution. Third parties must avoid the temptation to support or appear to support either of those in contention. They should adopt a counselling approach, as follows:

- listen actively;
- observe as well as listen;
- help people to understand and define the problem by asking pertinent, open-ended questions;
- recognize feelings and allow them to be expressed;
- help people to define problems for themselves;
- encourage people to explore alternative solutions;
- get people to develop their own implementation plans but provide advice and help if asked.

Conclusion

Conflict, as has been said, is in itself not to be deplored; it is an inevitable concomitant of progress and change. What is regrettable is the failure to use conflict constructively. Effective problem-solving and constructive confrontation both resolve conflicts and open up channels of discussion and cooperative action.

Many years ago, one of the pioneering writers on management, Mary Parker Follett,[2] wrote something on managing conflict that is as valid today as it was then: 'Differences can be made to contribute to the common cause if they are resolved by integration rather than domination or compromise.'

Endnotes

1 Ware, J and Barnes, L (1991) Managing interpersonal conflict, in *Managing People and Organizations*, ed J Gabarro, Harvard Business School Publications, Boston, MA

2 Follett, M P (1924) *Creative Experience*, Longmans Green, New York

How to manage a crisis 18

What is crisis management?

The phrase 'crisis management' was coined by Robert McNamara at the time of the Cuban missile crisis when he said: 'There is no longer any such thing as strategy, only crisis management.'

Crisis management situations happen in any organization where the pressure of events – external or internal – forces management into making urgent decisions. These arise because a crisis is a turning point or a time of danger and suspense, and, in this turbulent age, turning points and dangerous moments are always with us.

Crisis management can be defined as:

> The process of dealing with a pressurized situation in a way that plans, organizes, directs and controls a number of interrelated operations and guides the decision-making process of those in charge to a rapid but unhurried resolution of the acute problem faced by the organization.

Causes of crises

Crises are caused either by the actions of human beings or by natural disasters – fire, flood, earthquake and the like. If people are at the root of the crisis, they may be deliberately inflicting harm on the organization from outside or, also externally, they may have taken actions that indirectly create a major problem. Internally, crises can be caused deliberately by people attempting to enforce their point of view, accidentally by some colossal misjudgement, or by a long history of compounded errors.

Crises may, however, be no more than sudden, unforeseen events that perhaps could have been anticipated. To dismiss strategy, as McNamara did, is perhaps going too far, but Robert Burns did suggest that 'the best laid schemes o' mice an' men gang aft a-gley', and this is as true today as when he wrote it in the 18th century.

In an ideal world, crises would not happen. You would know where you want to go and you would get there, with only minor deviations along the way. Problems would have been foreseen and contingency plans made to deal with them. This, of course, is not the way things are in real life. Murphy's Law is always ready to strike again – if anything can go wrong it will.

Management crises

In management all sorts of crises can happen: a takeover bid, a collapse in the foreign exchange rate, a drug that has disastrous side-effects, a competitive product that suddenly appears on the market and wipes the floor with a market-leader brand, an innovation that renders a product obsolete, a sudden damaging strike, a dishonest senior executive who gets the company into the headlines, a fire or a flood, the departure of key members of the management team to competitors, and so on. The list is endless.

Tolstoy said of marriages: 'All happy families resemble one another, but each unhappy family is unhappy in its own way.' The same can be said of crises. Each crisis is a unique event and has to be dealt with accordingly. However, there are certain types of behaviour that are appropriate in all critical situations, and there are some general principles that can be followed in crises involving negotiation or conflict. There are also a number of crisis management techniques that are generally applicable, subject to modification to suit particular circumstances.

Crisis management techniques

The first thing to do when there is a potential crisis is to keep your finger on the pulse so that as soon as the pace hots up you can take pre-emptive action. At this stage, you have time to think, to consider contingency plans and to put them into effect.

If, however, in spite of all your efforts, you are faced with a crisis, the following is a checklist of the 10 steps you should take:

1   Sit back as coolly as you can and assess the situation. You may have to go through the analytical and thinking process five times as fast as usual, but do it. You need to establish:

- what exactly is happening;
- why it is happening;
- what is likely to happen unless something is done about it;
- how quickly you have to act to prevent further damage;
- who else is involved;
- who is likely to be involved;
- what resources you have – people, equipment, finance, back-up from other organizations, access to people with influence.

2   Draw up your preliminary plan of action – set it out step by step and prepare other contingency plans to deal with eventualities.

3   Line up a crisis management team to deal with the situation. Allocate roles and tasks and authorities to act (you may have to give emergency authority to some people).

4   Set up a crisis management centre (your office, the board room).

5   Set up a communications system so that you receive instant intelligence on what is happening and can put your messages across to the members of your team and anyone else whom you want to take action.

6   'Load shed' when you can, on the principle of the electrical system that sheds part of the load when the total load rises above a certain point. This means getting rid of any peripheral problems as quickly as possible.

7   Put items on the 'back burner'; in other words, relegate problems to a non-crisis area where they can be dealt with at leisure.

8   Prepare your detailed plans, which will include:

- timescales – act now or later;
- scope for a cooling-off period;
- longer-term solutions to be prepared and implemented at the right time;
- contingency plans to deal with new developments or emergencies.

9   Monitor continuously exactly what is happening. Ensure that you get the information you need fast so that you can react quickly but without panicking.

10   Evaluate actions and reactions continuously so that you can modify the plan and swiftly take corrective or pre-emptive steps.

Qualities of a crisis manager

Good crisis managers are decisive. They can react swiftly but their great skill is in being able to speed up the decision-making process. They will not miss out any of the 10 steps in the standard problem-solving, decision-making sequence:

1   define the situation;

2   specify objectives;

3   develop hypotheses;

4   gather the facts;

5   analyse the facts;

6   consider possible courses of action;

7   evaluate possible courses of action;

8   decide and implement;

9   monitor implementation;

10   evaluate outcomes and take steps to avoid a recurrence.

Effective crisis managers will get through these stages more quickly, using their own experience and intelligence and that of their team.

Crisis managers buy time by putting issues on the back burner, but, like all good managers, they can make things happen fast when they want to. They are good leaders – providing inspiration to their team, encouraging their efforts and giving them confidence in the successful outcome of the crisis management process.

Finally, and most important, they keep cool. They do not panic, they do not overreact, they do not lose their head. In fact, they deliberately slow down the pace, when they can, to give the impression that everything is under control and it is all going according to plan.

To sum up, crisis management is no more than good management under pressure. The adrenalin may flow faster but this concentrates the mind wonderfully. Good managers thrive under pressure and they are the good crisis managers.

How to manage projects   19

Project management is the planning, supervision and control of any activity or set of activities that leads to a defined outcome at a predetermined time and in accordance with specified performance or quality standards at a budgeted cost. It is concerned with deliverables – getting things done as required or promised. While delivering results on time is important, it is equally important to deliver them to meet the specification and within the projected cost.

Project management involves action planning – deciding *what* work is to be done, *why* the work needs to be done, *who* will do the work, *how much* it will cost, *when* it has to be completed (totally or stage by stage) and *where* it will be carried out.

The three main project management activities are project planning, setting up the project and project control.

Project planning

Initiation

Project planning starts with a definition of the objectives of the project. A business case has to be made. This means answering two basic questions:

- Why is this project needed?
- What benefits are expected from the project?

The answers to these questions should be quantified. The requirement could be spelled out in such terms as new systems or facilities to meet defined business needs, new plant required for new products, or improvements in productivity or quality. The benefits are expressed as revenues generated, productivity, quality or performance improvements, costs saved and return on investment.

Assessment

Projects involve investing resources – money and people. Investment appraisal techniques are used to ensure that the company's criteria for return on investment are satisfied. Cost–benefit analysis may be used to assess the degree to which the benefits justify the costs, time and number of people required by the project. This may mean identifying opportunity costs that establish whether a greater benefit would be obtained by investing the money or deploying the people on other projects or activities.

Performance specification

This sets out what the project is expected to do – how it should perform – and describes the details of the project's configuration or method of operation.

Project plan

The project plan sets out:

- the major operations in sequence – the main stages of the project;
- a breakdown where appropriate of each major operation into a sequence of subsidiary tasks;
- an analysis of the interrelationships and interdependencies of major and subsidiary tasks;
- an estimate of the time required to complete each major operation or stage;
- an assessment of the resources required – money, people, equipment and time;
- a procurement plan to obtain the necessary materials, systems and equipment;

- a human resource plan that defines how many people will be allocated to the project with different skills at each stage, and who is to be responsible for controlling the project as a whole and at each of the major stages or operations.

But project management is not just about piling extra resources in to get things completed on time. As Fred Brooks[1] discovered when he was with IBM, the project he was managing was falling badly behind schedule and more resources (ie programmers) were thrown at the task. But as this happened, the problems got worse, not better. Every time a programmer was added to the team the project fell further behind. The problem was the difficulty of coordinating the vastly increased resources. In his book on the subject he formulated Brooks' law: 'Adding manpower to a late project makes it later.'

Setting up the project

Setting up the project involves:

- obtaining and allocating resources;
- selecting and briefing the project management team;
- finalizing the project programme – defining each stage;
- defining and establishing control systems and reporting procedures (format and timing of progress reports);
- identifying key dates, stage by stage, for the project (milestones) and providing for milestone meetings to review progress and decide on any actions required.

Controlling the project

The three most important things to control are:

1 *time* – achievement of project plan as programme;
2 *quality* – achievement of project specifications;
3 *cost* – containment of costs within budget.

Project control is based on progress reports showing what is being achieved against the plan. The planned completion date, actual achievement and forecast completion date for each stage or operation are provided. The likelihood of delays, overruns or bottlenecks is thus established so that corrective action can be taken in good time. Control can be achieved by the use of Gantt or bar charts and by reference to network plans or critical path analyses.

Progress meetings should be held at predetermined intervals. These can be treated as 'milestone' meetings when they are timed to coincide with the key stages of the project.

10 steps to effective project management

1 Specify objectives and deliverables.

2 Carry out cost–benefit analysis or investment appraisal to justify project.

3 Determine:

- what should be done;
- who does what;
- when it should be done (broken down into stages);
- how much it should cost.

4 Define resource requirements (people, money, materials, systems, equipment, etc).

5 Prepare programme – identify stages.

6 Define methods of control – charts, network analysis, progress reports, progress (milestone) meetings.

7 Ensure that everyone knows what is expected of them and has the resources required.

8 Monitor progress continuously against the plan as well as at formal meetings.

9 Take corrective action as required; for example, reallocating resources.

10 Evaluate the end result against the objectives and deliverables.

Endnote

1 Brooks, F P (1974) *The Mythical Man-Month: Essays on software engineering*, Addison Wesley, Reading, MA

How to manage risk

20

Risk management is concerned with avoiding unacceptable risks and managing existing risks in order to minimize any harmful impact they may make. Research carried out by the Economist Intelligence Unit amongst 3,000 executives showed that only 5 per cent of them were absolutely confident that their risk control systems were successfully identifying, evaluating, minimizing and managing all the potential significant risks affecting their business.

Risk management is influenced by two laws:

1 *Murphy's Law*, which states that if anything can go wrong it will.

2 *The law of unintended consequences*; an intervention in a complex system tends to create unanticipated and often undesirable outcomes.

Risks may be purely financial – what is the chance of an investment paying off? But the risks that destroyed Arthur Anderson, Barings, Enron and Lehman Brothers arose because of faults in management control, inadequate systems and staff negligence as well as unacceptable behaviour. An organization may sustain losses by failing to hedge its positions in the futures market. This may be because an inexperienced manager was given responsibility for the task and the company did not exercise reasonable supervision of that manager's activities. Public utilities may face regulatory notices and risks arising from political decisions, and these must be anticipated. Auditors must be aware of the risks they take when, if they are negligent, their audit report does not represent 'a full and fair view'. Overseas sales may be affected by political risks and a software firm has to be prepared for the risk that a competitor will produce a better product. A company that is a market leader may run the risk of being threatened by competitors – to what extent does the company monitor the competition, regularly assess customer requirements and seek improvements in the product or level of service to maintain a competitive edge? A business may rely on one customer for 80 per cent of its sales. What happens if this customer looks elsewhere? How big is this risk? What can be done to lessen it?

These situations and the questions that arise from them are all matters that should be dealt with by a systematic approach to risk management.

Categories of risk

The categories of risk are:

- *Commercial risk* – increased competition, better products or services available elsewhere, price cutting by competition, problems with suppliers, key customers failing or switching their business elsewhere.

- *Financial risk* – failed investments, fraud, default, poor liquidity, fall in market prices.

- *Economic risk* – recession in the United Kingdom or overseas markets, adverse exchange movements, worldwide decline in prices.

- *Political risk* – adverse political decisions (eg legislation, tax changes, regulatory changes, Office of Fair Trading investigations).

- *Technological development* – new developments making the company's products or services obsolete.

- *Health and safety* – the risk of illness, accidents or injuries at work.

- *Natural disasters* – fire, flood, riots, etc.

- *Crime* – embezzlement, fraud, computer crime, industrial espionage.

- *Legal* – the risk of successful actions against the company causing loss of money and reputation.
- *Fashion* – changes in fashion affecting demand.

Minimizing risk

The main ways to minimize risk are:

- Institute financial controls to prevent fraud.
- Set up compliance arrangements to ensure that regulations are adhered to.
- Monitor key transactions or those above a certain value and the people that make them to ensure that they are carried out in accordance with policies and procedures and do not entail undue risk.
- Insure against such risks as a major customer becoming insolvent, natural disasters or a country to which the company is exporting imposing currency restrictions that prevent payment.
- Diversify into products or services that have a different risk profile; avoid relying too much on one supplier.
- Hedge – take action that will provide compensation if risk occurs. The most typical area where hedging takes place is foreign currency transactions, which might involve buying the currency in advance. If the business is vulnerable to a sudden fall in the stock market, an option can be bought to provide funds if this happens. If the business is vulnerable to one set of factors, it can buy or acquire an interest in a business that would prosper from such factors.

Managing risk

The approaches to managing risk are:

- Recognize that risk assessment is a continuous activity – you cannot take the risk of not assessing risk.

- Make risk assessment and management a major concern of the board and top management.

- Ensure that everyone in the organization knows that they are in the business of identifying, reporting on and managing risks.

- Focus on the avoidance of unacceptable business risks, followed by the management of other business risks to reduce them to an acceptable level.

- Formulate a business risk controls policy and ensure that everyone knows and understands it.

- Anticipate business risk at the source and monitor risk controls continuously.

- Remember that the primary source of business risk is ineffective processes and controls rather than ineffective people.

How to manage stress

21

You become stressed when you experience more pressure, frustration, or a higher level of emotional demand than you can handle. An acceptable degree of pressure can be a good thing. It can stimulate and motivate you. Some people thrive on it. They respond to challenges that others would find hard to bear.

Pressures include: achieving performance expectations; meeting deadlines; coping with an excessive workload; dealing with difficult bosses, colleagues, clients, customers or subordinates, including bullying; problems of achieving a satisfactory work–life balance (reconciling the demands of work with family responsibilities or outside interests); and role ambiguity (lack of understanding of what is expected).

Pressure is fine as long as it does not build up to too high a level. Up to a point it will motivate and improve performance but it then turns into stress and results in a decline in performance as illustrated in Figure 21.1.

The important thing to remember is that the ability to withstand pressure varies: one person's stimulating amount of pressure is another person's stress. But this suggests that although some people may temperamentally be more prone to suffer from stress, there is some scope to manage or limit stress, bearing in mind that it is often self-imposed.

Symptoms of stress

The symptoms of stress that you can observe in others or yourself include inability to cope with the demands of the job (which creates more stress), tiredness, lethargy, lack of enthusiasm and bad temper.

Figure 21.1   How pressure becomes stress

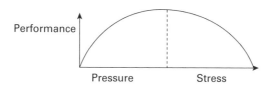

Managing stress in others

What the organization can do

Organizations can manage stress by developing processes and policies that can be implemented by line managers and specialist staff. These include:

- clarifying roles to reduce role ambiguity and give people more autonomy;
- setting reasonable and achievable performance standards;
- establishing performance management processes that encourage a dialogue about work and its pressures between managers and their staff;
- giving individuals the opportunity to obtain professional counselling;
- developing anti-bullying policies;
- developing work–life balance policies that take account of the pressures on employees as parents, partners or carers, and that can include provisions such as special leave or flexible working hours.

What you can do

To manage stress in others you need to do the following:

- Be aware of organizational policies and procedures as set out above, and be prepared to implement them for your own staff.

- Tailor your demands on people according to their capacities – it is a good idea to agree stretching targets but they must be achievable (with effort but without undue stress) by the individual concerned.

- Look out for symptoms of stress and try to establish the cause as the basis for alleviating them.

- If an individual is under stress because of undue pressure, try to adjust demands to a more reasonable level, possibly by redesigning the job or transferring duties to someone else.

- Be prepared to listen and respond to individuals who complain of being over-stressed – you don't have to accept what they say but you should certainly hear them out.

Managing your own stress

If you feel that you are unduly stressed, here are 10 things you can do:

1 Try to establish why you are stressed – are there any specific causes or is it a general feeling that the work is getting on top of you?

2 Talk to someone about it – your boss (if likely to be sympathetic), colleagues, HR, friends, your partner.

3 If the stress is serious, ask if the organization can provide advice from a professional counsellor.

4 Discuss your workloads and deadlines with your boss to see if they can be alleviated in any way.

5 Consider whether there is any scope to delegate more work to your staff.

6 Decide what is beyond your control and put it firmly to one side. Focus on what is within your sphere of influence and get on with it.

7 Take time off during the day – relax (switch off) for a few minutes over a cup of coffee with your colleagues.

8 Don't work excessive hours.

9 Don't take work home.

10 Take regular exercise.

How to manage time

22

I wasted time, and now doth time waste me. RICHARD II

If you were told by your chief executive officer that you were needed for a special assignment that would mean working directly under him, give you the opportunity to deal with strategic issues, broaden your experience and provide you with excellent promotion prospects, would you take it? The answer would, of course, be yes. If, however, you were told that you would spend one day a week on this assignment and carry out your present duties in the remaining four days, would you still accept the job? Of course you would. But you would be admitting that you could, if you organized yourself better, do your existing work in four-fifths of the time you spend on it at the moment.

To recover that one-fifth or more, you need to think systematically about how you use your time. You can then take steps to organize yourself better and to get other people to help or at least not to hinder you.

Analysis

The first thing to do is to find out where there is scope for improving your use of time.

Your job

Start with your job – the tasks you have to carry out and the objectives you are there to achieve. Try to establish an order of priority between your tasks and among your objectives.

It is more difficult to do this if you have a number of potentially conflicting areas of responsibility. A good example of this was a director of administration who had a ragbag of responsibilities including property, office services and staff. He had perpetual problems with conflicting priorities and, all too frequently, at the end of the day he would say to himself: 'I have wasted my time, I have achieved next to nothing.'

He took a day off to think things through and realized that he had to take a broad view before getting into detail. He felt that if he could sort out the relative importance of his objectives he would be in a better position to attach priorities to his tasks.

Having done this, he could rely on preventive maintenance to reduce problems. But when a crisis did occur – which was inevitable in his area – he could concentrate on fire-fighting in one place without having to worry about what was going on elsewhere.

His second objective, therefore, was to give himself sufficient free time to concentrate on major problems so that he could react swiftly to them. He then classified the sorts of issues that could arise and decided which could safely be delegated to others and which he should deal with himself. He was thus prepared to allocate priorities as the problems landed on his desk and to select the serious ones to deal with himself, knowing that the administrative system would go on without interruption.

How you spend your time

Having sorted out your main priorities you should analyse in more detail how you spend your time. This will identify time-consuming activities and indicate where there are problems as well as possible solutions to them.

The best way to analyse time is to keep a diary. You can do this electronically using Microsoft Outlook organizing software. Do this for a week, or preferably two or three, as one week may not provide a typical picture. Divide the day into 15-minute sections and note down what you did in each period. Against each space, summarize how effectively you spent your time by writing V for valuable, D for doubtful and U for useless. If you want to make more refined judgements give your ratings pluses or minuses.

For example:

Table 22.1   Time management diary

Time	Task	Rating
9.00–9.30	Dealt with new e-mails and incoming mail	V
		V
9.30–9.45	Discussed admin problem	D
9.45–10.00	Discussed admin problem	D
10.00–10.15	Deputized at meeting	U
10.15–10.30	Deputized at meeting	U
10.30–10.45	Deputized at meeting	U
10.45–11.00	Deputized at meeting	U

At the end of the week analyse your time under the following headings:

- reading;
- writing;
- dictating;
- sending and receiving e-mails;
- telephoning;
- dealing with people (individuals or groups);
- attending meetings;
- travelling;
- other (specify).

Analyse also the VDU ratings of the worth of each activity under each heading. This analysis will provide you with the information you need to spot any weaknesses in the way in which you manage time.

Use the time-consumer's checklist (Table 22.2) at the end of this chapter to identify problems and possible remedies.

Organizing yourself

Such an analysis will usually throw up weaknesses in the way you plan your work and establish your priorities. You have to fit the tasks you must complete into the time available to complete them, and get them done in order of importance.

Some people find it difficult, if not impossible, to plan their work ahead. They find that they work best if they have to achieve almost impossible deadlines. Working under pressure concentrates the mind wonderfully, they say. Journalists are a case in point.

But ordinary mortals, who work under a variety of conflicting pressures, cannot rely upon crisis action to get them out of logjams of work. For most of us it is better to try to minimize the need to work under exceptional pressure by a little attention to the organization of our week or day. At the very least you should use your diary for long-range planning, organize your weekly activities in broad outline and plan each day in some detail.

Use the diary

Attempt to leave at least one day a week free of meetings and avoid filling any day with appointments. In other words, leave blocks of unallocated time for planning, thinking, reading, writing and dealing with the unexpected.

Weekly organizer

Sit down at the beginning of each week with your diary and plan how you are going to spend your time. Assess each of your projects or tasks and work out priorities. Leave blocks of time for dealing with e-mails and other correspondence and for seeing people. Try to preserve one free day, or at least half a day, if it is at all possible.

If it helps you to put everything down on paper, draw up a simple weekly organizer form and record what you intend to do each morning, afternoon and, if it's work, evening.

Daily organizer

At the beginning of each day, consult your diary to check on your plans and commitments. Refer to the previous day's organizer to find out what is outstanding. Inspect your pending tray, in-tray and incoming e-mails to check on what remains and what has just arrived.

Then write down the things to do:

1 meetings or interviews;

2 respond to e-mails;

3 telephone calls;

4 tasks in order of priority:

   A – must be done today;

   B – ideally should be done today but could be left until tomorrow;

   C – can be dealt with later.

Plan broadly when you are going to fit your A and B priority tasks into the day. Tick off your tasks as they have been completed. Retain the list to consult the next day.

You can use your electronic organizer for this purpose. Many successful time managers only use a blank sheet of paper, but a simple form that you can use is shown below.

Organizing other people

Your first task is to organize yourself, but other people can help if you can guide and encourage them. They include your PA, boss, colleagues, subordinates and outside contacts.

Your PA

A PA can be a great help: sorting incoming mail into what needs immediate attention and what can be looked at later; managing appointments within your guidelines; keeping unwanted callers at bay; intercepting telephone calls; dealing with routine or even semi-routine correspondence; sorting and arranging your papers and the filing system for easy accessibility; getting people on the telephone for you, and so on. The list is almost endless. Every efficient boss will recognize that he or she depends a lot on an efficient PA.

Your boss

Your boss can waste your time with over-long meetings, needless interruptions, trivial requests and general nitpicking. Maybe there is nothing you can do about this. But you can learn how to avoid doing the same to your own staff.

On your own behalf you can cultivate the polite art of cutting short tedious discussions. Such formulas as 'I hope you feel we have cleared up this problem – I'll get out of your hair now and get things moving' are useful. And you might be able, subtly, to indicate that your boss is going to get better performance from you if he leaves you alone. It's difficult but it's worth trying.

Your colleagues

Try to educate them to avoid unnecessary interruptions. Don't anger them by shutting them out when they have something urgent to discuss. But if it can wait, get them to agree to meet you later at a fixed time. Try to avoid indulging in too many pleasantries over the telephone. Be brisk but not brusque. Try to persuade them not to deluge you with unnecessary e-mails.

Your subordinates

You will save a lot of time with your subordinates if you systematically decide what work you can delegate to them. You save even more time if you delegate clearly and spell out how and when you want them to report back.

An 'open door' policy is fine in theory but time-wasting in practice. Learn to say no to subordinates who want to see you when you are engaged on more important business. But always give them a time when they can see you – and stick to it.

Talking generally to your staff about their job and outside interests can be time well spent if it helps to increase mutual understanding and respect. Allow for this in your schedule and be prepared to extend business discussions into broader matters when the opportunity arises. But don't overdo it.

Outside contacts

The same rules apply to outside contacts. Prevent them from seeing you without an appointment. Ask your PA to block unwanted telephone calls. Brief your contacts on what you expect from them and when meetings should be arranged.

Dealing with time problems

Table 22.2   Time-consumer's checklist

Problem	Possible remedies
TASKS	
1 Work piling up	• Set priorities. • Set deadlines. • Make realistic time estimates – most people underestimate; add 20 per cent to your first guess.
2 Trying to do too much at once	• Set priorities. • Do one thing at a time. • Learn to say no to yourself as well as other people.
3 Getting involved in too much detail	• Delegate more.
4 Postponing unpleasant tasks	• Set a timetable and stick to it. • Get unpleasant tasks over with quickly – you will feel better afterwards.
5 Insufficient time to think	• Reserve blocks of time – part of a day or week – for thinking. No paperwork, no interruptions.

(continued)

Table 22.2 (*Continued*)

Problem	Possible remedies
PEOPLE	
6 Constant interruptions from people calling into your office	• Use PA to keep unwanted visitors out. • Make appointments and see that people stick to them. • Reserve block times when you are not to be interrupted.
7 Constant telephone interruptions	• Get your PA to intercept and, where appropriate, divert calls. • State firmly that you will call back when convenient.
8 Too much time spent in conversation	• Decide in advance what you want to achieve when you meet someone, and keep pleasantries to a minimum at the beginning and end. • Concentrate on keeping yourself and the other person to the point – it is too easy to divert or be diverted. • Learn how to end meetings quickly but not too brusquely.
PAPERWORK	
9 Flooded with incoming paper	• Get your PA to sort it into three folders: action now, action later, information. • Take yourself off the circulation list of useless information. • Only ask for written memos and reports when you really need them. • Encourage people to present information and reports clearly and succinctly. • Ask for summaries rather than the whole report. • Take a course in rapid reading.

(*continued*)

Table 22.2   (*Continued*)

Problem	Possible remedies
PAPERWORK	
10 Too many e-mails to deal with	• If it really matters go and talk to them. • Rediscover the power of a phone call. • Use handwritten notes. • Get yourself off distribution lists. • Use Out of the Office Auto-reply more. • Check your inbox only once or twice a day. • Practise sending a succinct reply – 'yes/no/let's talk'.
11 Too many letters/memos to write or dictate	• Use the telephone or e-mail more. • Avoid individually typed acknowledgements.
12 Paperwork piling up	• Do it now. • Set aside the first half hour or so in the day to deal with urgent correspondence. • Leave a period at the end of the day for less urgent reading. • Aim to clear at least 90 per cent of the paper on your desk or messages in your inbox every day.
13 Lost or mislaid papers	• Arrange, or get your PA to organize, papers on current projects in separate, easily accessible folders. • Don't hang on to papers in your pending tray – clear it daily. • Set up a filing and retrieval system which will enable you to get at papers easily. • Ensure that your PA keeps a day book of correspondence as a last-resort method of turning up papers. • Keep a tidy desk.

(*continued*)

Table 22.2 (*Continued*)

Problem	Possible remedies
MEETINGS	
14 Too much time spent in meetings	• If you set up the meeting: avoid regular meetings when there is nothing that needs saying; review all the meetings you hold and eliminate as many as you can. • Get yourself taken off committees if your presence is not essential or someone else is more appropriate. • As chairperson: set limits for the duration of meetings and keep to them; cut out waffle and repetition; allow discussion but insist on making progress; have a logical agenda and stick to it. • As a member: don't waffle; don't talk for the sake of talking; don't waste time scoring points or boosting your ego.
TRAVELLING	
15 Too much time spent on travelling	• Use the phone or post. • Send someone else. • Ask yourself, every time you plan to go anywhere: 'Is my journey really necessary?' • Plan the quickest way – air, rail or car.

How to persuade

23

A manager's job is 60 per cent getting it right and 40 per cent putting it across. Managers spend a lot of time persuading other people to accept their ideas and suggestions. Persuasion is just another word for selling. You may feel that good ideas should sell themselves, but life is not like that. Everyone resists change and anything new is certain to be treated with suspicion. So it's worth learning a few simple rules that will help you to sell your ideas more effectively.

10 rules for effective persuasion

1   Define the problem. Determine whether the problem is a misunderstanding (a failure to understand each other accurately) or a true disagreement (a failure to agree even when both parties understand one another). It is not necessarily possible to resolve a true disagreement by understanding each other better. People generally believe that an argument is a battle to understand who is correct. More often, it is a battle to decide who is more stubborn.

2   Define your objective and get the facts. Decide what you want to achieve and why. Assemble all the facts you need to support your case. Eliminate emotional arguments so that you and others can judge the proposition on the facts alone.

3   Find out what the other party wants. The key to all persuasion is to see your proposition from the other person's point of view. Find out how he or she looks at things. Establish what he or she needs and wants.

4 Accentuate the benefits. Present your case in a way that highlights the benefits to the other party, or at least reduces any objections or fears.

5 Predict the other person's response. Everything we say should be focused on that likely response. Anticipate objections by asking yourself how the other party might react negatively to your proposition and thinking up ways of responding to him or her.

6 Create the other person's next move. It is not a question of deciding what we want to do but what we want the other person to do. Your goal is to get results.

7 Convince people by reference to their own perceptions. People decide what to do on the basis of their own perceptions, not yours.

8 Prepare a simple and attractive proposition. Make it as straightforward as possible. Present the case 'sunny side up', emphasizing its benefits. Break the problem into manageable pieces and deal with them one step at a time.

9 Make the other person a party to your ideas. Get him or her to contribute. Find some common ground so that you can start with agreement. Don't try to defeat the other person in an argument – you will only antagonize him or her.

10 Clinch and take action. Choose the right moment to clinch the proposal – don't prolong the discussion and risk losing it. But follow up promptly.

How to negotiate

24

Negotiation is the process of coming to terms and, in so doing, getting the best deal possible for your firm, your union or yourself.

Negotiations involve a conflict of interest. Sellers prefer a high price to a low one and buyers prefer a low price to a high one. Unions want the highest settlement they can get, management wants the lowest. It can be a zero-sum game – what one side gains the other loses. No one likes to lose, so there is conflict, which has to be managed if an amicable agreement is to be achieved. And negotiators do, or should, try to end up on friendly terms, whatever differences of opinion have occurred on the way. After all, they may well meet again.

Another important feature of negotiations is that they take place in an atmosphere of uncertainty. Neither side necessarily knows what the other wants or will give.

There are two main types of negotiation – business and trade union.

Business negotiations

Business negotiations are mainly about the price and the terms for supplying goods or services.

In their simplest form they are no more than a haggle between buyer and seller, much the same as what happens when you trade in your car for a new one. At their more complex, they concern a package in which a number of extras are on offer along with the basic product. Sellers can usually offer a range of prices to suit the needs of the buyer: an 'ex-works' price, a delivered price, an installed price and a price that includes service. Various methods of staging payments or providing credit may also be offered.

Negotiations of this type usually start with the buyer producing a specification. The seller then produces a proposal and negotiation starts. The seller will have included a negotiating margin in the proposal and will be prepared to vary the price according to the package required.

Business negotiations are usually conducted in a friendly manner, and that's your major problem. You can too easily be seduced into accepting a less than satisfactory deal by the blandishments of the negotiator.

Trade union negotiations

Trade union negotiations can be much tougher. They may involve a simple pay settlement, but usually they involve a package. Extra benefits will be at issue, and can be traded for concessions if need be.

In this type of negotiation, both parties are probably quite clear as to the maximum they will give or the minimum they will accept. They will have predetermined their opening demands and offers, and their shopping list of extras will have been analysed to determine which points can be conceded in return for some benefit.

There are a number of bargaining conventions used in union negotiations, of which the following are the most generally accepted:

- Whatever happens during the bargaining, both parties hope to come to a settlement.

- Attacks, hard words, threats and (controlled) losses of temper are treated by both sides as legitimate tactics and should not be allowed to shake either party's belief in the other's integrity, or their desire to settle without taking drastic action.

- Off-the-record discussions (beneficial as a means of probing attitudes and intentions) should not be referred to specifically in formal bargaining sessions, unless both sides agree in advance.

- Each side should be prepared to move from its original position.

- It is normal, although not inevitable, for the negotiation to proceed with a series of offers and counter-offers that lead steadily towards a settlement.

- Concessions, once made, cannot be withdrawn.

- Firm offers must not be withdrawn, although it is legitimate to make and withdraw conditional offers.

- A third party should not be brought in until both parties are agreed that no further progress would be made without one.

- The final agreement should mean exactly what it says. There should be no trickery and the terms agreed should be implemented without amendment.

- If possible, the final settlement should be framed so that both sides can save face and credibility.

The process of negotiation

Stage 1: Preparation – setting objectives (or drawing up specifications), assembling data, and deciding on negotiating strategy.

Stage 2: Opening – negotiators reveal their initial bargaining positions to their opposite numbers.

Stage 3: Bargaining – negotiators attempt to reach the most advantageous position in discussion with another party through a process of offer and counter-offer.

Stage 4: Closing – each party judges whether the other side is determined to stick to its position or will settle for a compromise. The final moves are made. It is during this stage that final 'trade-offs' may lead to a settlement.

Negotiating tactics

Preparation

1 Define your bargaining objectives as follows:

- ideal – the best you can hope to achieve;

- minimum – the least you would be prepared to settle for;

- target – what you are going to try for and believe, realistically, you have a good chance of achieving.

2 Consider how you might build up a package that would allow concessions to be exchanged. For example, could you accept a higher price for a concession on payment terms, or increase a pay offer if the union agrees to remove a restrictive practice?

3 Assess what the other party wants or is prepared to offer. For example, if you are a manufacturer negotiating terms with a store, it pays to know, say, that the buyer is constrained by company policy that insists on a three-times mark-up. Knowing the retail price that the store will want to charge, you will have a good idea of the maximum the buyer will pay. You can then judge whether you should press for a larger order to justify a lower selling price than you would normally accept.

In a typical wage negotiation, the union or representative body making the claim will come to the table with a predetermined target, minimum and opening claims. Similarly, you, as the employer, will have your own target, maximum and opening offer. The difference between their claim and your offer is the negotiating range. If your maximum exceeds their minimum this will indicate the settlement zone. This is demonstrated in Figure 24.1. In this example the chance of settlement without too much trouble is fairly high. It is when your maximum is less than their minimum, as in Figure 24.2, that the trouble starts.

4 Decide on your strategy and tactics – your opening offer, the steps you are going to take, the concessions you are prepared to offer and the arguments you are going to use.

5 Collect the facts needed to support your case.

6 Assemble any documents you need, such as standard contract terms.

In a trade union negotiation:

1 Select the negotiating team. This should never have fewer than two members, and for major negotiations should have three or more: one to take the lead, one to take notes and feed the negotiator with any supporting information needed, and the others to observe their opposite numbers and play a specific part in negotiations in accordance with their brief.

Figure 24.1 Negotiating range with a settlement zone

Figure 24.2 Negotiating range without a settlement zone

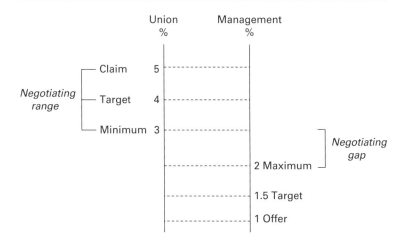

2 Brief the members of the negotiating team on their roles and the negotiating strategy and tactics that are to be adopted. If appropriate, prepared statements or arguments should be issued at this stage to be used as required by the strategic plan.

3 Rehearse the members of the team in their roles. They can be asked to repeat their points to other members and deal with responses from them; or someone can act as devil's advocate and force the leader or other members of the team to handle awkward points or negotiating ploys.

At this stage it may be possible to meet your opponents informally to sound out their position, while they sound out yours. You can use such a session as an 'early warning' system to get your opponents to modify their initial demands by convincing them of the strength of your own position or your determination to resist.

Opening

Your tactics when opening the negotiation should be to:

- open realistically and move moderately;
- challenge your opponents' position as it stands, but on no account limit their ability to move;
- explore attitudes, ask questions, observe behaviour and, above all, listen; assess your opponents' strengths and weaknesses, their tactics and the extent to which they may be bluffing;
- make no concessions of any kind at this stage;
- be non-committal about proposals and explanations (do not talk too much).

Bargaining

Your aim is to narrow the gap between the two initial positions and to persuade your opponents that your case is so strong that they must accept less than they had planned. You should:

- always make conditional proposals: 'If you will do this I will consider doing that';
- never make one-sided concessions – always trade-off against a concession from the other party: 'If I concede X then I expect you to concede Y.'

- negotiate on the whole package – never allow your opponents to pick you off item by item; keep all the issues open so as to extract the maximum benefit from potential trade-offs.

Reading the signals

During the bargaining stage you must be sensitive to any signals made by the other party. Every time they make a conditional statement it shows that they are prepared to move. Explore the possibilities with questions. Try to get behind what people say and understand what they really mean. For example:

Table 24.1   What they say and what they mean!

What they say	What they mean
That is as far as I can go.	I might be able to persuade my boss to go further.
We don't usually give more than 5 per cent discount.	We're prepared to give more if you give us something in return.
Let's think about that point.	I'm prepared to negotiate.
I need notice of that question.	It's difficult but not impossible. Try again.
It will be very difficult for us to meet that requirement.	It's not impossible but we'll want a trade-off.
I shall certainly consider your offer.	I am going to accept it but I don't want to appear to be too easy a touch.
This is our standard contract.	We're prepared to negotiate on the terms.
We're prepared to offer you £x for y units.	The price is negotiable.
That's my final offer.	My boss might go further if pushed or if it is worth her while.
We couldn't meet your delivery requirements at that price.	I will negotiate on delivery or price.

Arguing

During the bargaining stage, much of your time will be spent arguing. Clear thinking (see Chapter 46) will help you to present your case and expose the fallacies in your opponent's arguments.

You should also consider the manner in which you argue. You are not there to beat your opponent into the ground. In fact, in the interests of future good relationships (which will benefit you as well as your opponent) it is wise to leave an escape route. As a leading trade unionist said: 'Always leave the other fellow the price of his bus ticket home.'

Avoid brow-beating your opponent. Disagree firmly, but don't shoot him down. Don't try to make your opponent look small. Score points, if you must, to discredit arguments or expose fallacious reasoning but never in order to discredit him or her as a person. If you indulge in personal attacks or abuse, your opponents will close ranks.

To argue effectively you must be prepared to listen both to the stated and to the implied points made by your opponent. Don't talk too much yourself; it will prevent you reading signals, and you may give too much away. Wherever you can, challenge your opponent to justify the case on an item-by-item basis. Put the onus on him or her by questioning for clarification. Answer a question with another question if you want time to consider.

Argue calmly and without emotion, but emphasize the points you really want to ram home either by raising your voice slightly and slowing down to highlight your argument, or by repetition.

Control your anger. Express yourself strongly, by all means, but you will lose everything if you lose your temper.

Always remember that you are not trying to win at all costs. If your opponent wants something that you cannot give, don't just say no. Offer an alternative package. If your opponent is asking for a higher specification than you normally provide for the price and wants a delivery date that you cannot meet without incurring extra overtime costs, say that you can meet the specifications and the delivery deadline as long as the other side is prepared to cover the costs.

Gambits

There are a number of standard bargaining gambits. Here are a few of the more common ones:

- *Uttering threats* – 'Agree to what I want or I'll call out the lads', or 'I'll take my custom elsewhere.' Don't overreact to such threats; simply treat them as part of the normal cut and thrust of negotiation and continue to address the point at issue.

- *No negotiation under duress* – 'We refuse to discuss your claim unless and until you cancel your overtime ban.' An excellent approach, if you can get away with it.

- *It will reflect badly on you* – 'Do you really want to get the reputation of being a heartless employer?' This is an emotional appeal and, as such, should be discounted.

- *The bluff direct* – 'I have two or three quotations lower than yours.' The answer to this gambit is to call your opponent's bluff – 'What are they offering for the price?' 'OK, why not accept them, why bother talking to me?'

- *The leading question* – 'Do you think it is a good idea to reward people according to merit?' 'Yes.' 'Then why do you insist on retaining this fixed incremental scheme that benefits everybody irrespective of how well they've done?' Never fall for a leading question.

- *The piecemeal or 'salami' technique* – In this your opponent will try to pick off the items one by one. 'That's the price agreed, now we can deliver in three months, OK?' 'Right, we've agreed the delivery terms, now this is how we charge for maintenance.' Always negotiate the whole package. Don't allow yourself to be railroaded into a piecemeal approach.

- *The 'yes, but...' approach* – 'Yes, we agree to accept an increase of 8 per cent, but before we can agree to everything there is this other problem of compensation for redundancy we must tackle.' To avoid being caught in a 'yes, but' trap, always make offers on one part of a package conditional on accepting another part: 'We are prepared to consider a 4 per cent offer but only if you agree to drop your claim for enhanced redundancy pay.'

Closing

When and how you close depends on your assessment of the strength of your opponent's case and his or her determination to see it through. You may close by:

- Making a concession, preferably a minor one, and trading it off against an agreement to settle. The concession can be offered more positively than at the bargaining stage: 'If you will agree to settle at X, I will concede Y.'

- Doing a deal: you might split the difference, or bring in something new – such as extending the settlement timescale, agreeing to back payments, phasing increases, making a joint declaration of intent to do something in the future (for example to introduce a productivity plan), or offering an incentive discount.

- Summarizing what has happened to date, emphasizing the concessions that have been made and the extent to which you have moved, and stating that you have reached your final position.

- Applying pressure through a threat of the consequences that will follow if your offer is not accepted.

- Giving your opponent a choice between two courses of action.

Do not say something is a final offer unless you mean it. If it is not really your final offer and your opponent calls your bluff, you will have to make further concessions and your credibility will be undermined. Your opponent will, of course, attempt to force you into revealing how close you are to your final position. Do not allow yourself to be hurried into this. If you want to avoid committing yourself and thus devaluing the word 'final', state as positively as you can that this is as far as you are prepared to go.

How to run a meeting

25

When you think how many committees exist and how many meetings are held in any organization, it is remarkable how hard it is to find anyone who has a good word to say about them.

It has been said that committees are made up of the unfit appointed by the incompetent to do the unnecessary, and that a camel is a horse designed by a committee. Experience of badly organized and pointless meetings is so widespread that, for many people, these cynical comments come very close to the truth. To run meetings successfully you must take account of the dos and don'ts concerning their creation and operation and ensure that there is an effective chairperson.

Dos and don'ts of meetings

Table 25.1   Dos and don'ts of meetings

Do	Don't
• Use a meeting if the information or the judgement is too great for one person.	• Use a meeting if one person can do the job better.
• Set up committees only when it is essential to assemble people with different viewpoints in one place at one time.	• Set up a committee if you want sharp, clear responsibility.
• Appoint a chairperson who is going to be able to control the meeting and get the best out of it.	• Use a committee to administrate anything.
	• Use a meeting or committee if you need speedy action.

(continued)

Table 25.1 (*Continued*)

Do	Don't
• Put people with different backgrounds who can contribute ideas on the committee.	• Appoint a bigger committee than you need – over 10 people can become unwieldy.
• Tell committees what they are to do and what their authority is.	• Hold unnecessary meetings – it may be good to meet regularly on the first Friday of every month but it may be even better to meet only when you have something to discuss.
• Be explicit about when you want the meeting to report back.	
• Use meetings where they work best – reviewing or developing policies, coordinating decisions, ensuring that all concerned with a programme are consulted and kept informed.	
• Wind up committees as soon as they have served their purpose.	

Chairing meetings

The success or failure of a meeting largely depends on the chairman. If you are chairing a meeting, this is what you must do.

Prior to the meeting

Before the meeting starts, ensure that it has proper terms of reference and that the members are briefed on what to expect and what they should be prepared to contribute. Plan the agenda to provide for a structured meeting, covering all the issues in a logical order. Prepare and issue briefing papers that will structure the meeting and spell out the background, thus saving time going into detail or reviewing purely factual information during the meeting.

During the meeting

- Start by clearly defining the objective of the meeting, setting a timescale that you intend to keep.

- Go through each item of the agenda in turn, ensuring that a firm conclusion is reached and recorded.

- Initiate the discussion on each item by setting the scene very briefly and asking for contributions – ask for answers to specific questions (which you should have prepared in advance) or you may refer the matter first to a member of the meeting who can make the best initial contribution (ideally, you should have briefed that individual in advance).

- Invite contributions from other members of the meeting, taking care not to allow anyone to dominate the discussions.

- Bring people back to order if they drift from the point.

- If there is too much talk, remind members that they are there to make progress.

- Encourage the expression of different points of view and avoid crushing anyone too obviously if they have not made a sensible comment.

- Allow disagreement between members of the meeting but step in smartly if the atmosphere becomes too contentious.

- Chip in with questions or brief comments from time to time, but do not dominate the discussion.

- At appropriate moments during the meeting summarize the discussion, express views on where the committee has got to and outline your perception of the interim or final decision that has been made. Then check that the meeting agrees, amending the conclusion as necessary, and ensure that the decision is recorded exactly as made.

- Summarize what has been achieved at the end of the meeting, indicating who has to do what by when.

- If a further meeting is needed, agree the purpose of the meeting and what has to be done by those present before it takes place.

- Remember that meetings can run in phases. For example, they start with an explanation, continue with a discussion of pros and cons, run into a sidetrack and have to be brought into line, generate more heat than light because of contending points of view, and eventually reach a point where you realize a decision has to be taken.

- If you are chairing a meeting you may have to change your style accordingly. You may have to be decisive in bringing people to the point or business to a close, relaxed if you want to allow the discussion to keep going, or persuasive in order to draw people into the discussion.

How to be an effective member of a meeting

If you are a member of a meeting you should:

- Prepare thoroughly – have all the facts at your fingertips, with any supporting data you need.

- Make your points clearly, succinctly and positively – try to resist the temptation of talking too much.

- Contribute fully but only when you have something to say.

- Keep your powder dry if you are not leading the discussion or if it is a subject you are not knowledgeable about. Listen, observe and save your arguments until you can make a really telling point. Don't plunge in too quickly or comprehensively – there may be other compelling arguments.

- If you are not too sure of your ground, avoid making statements such as 'I think we must do this'. Instead, pose a question to the chairman or other member of the meeting such as 'Do you think there is a case for doing this?'

- Be prepared to argue your case firmly, but don't persist in fighting for a lost cause. Don't retire in a sulk because you cannot get your own way; accept defeat gracefully.

- Remember that if you are defeated in committee, there may still be a chance for you to fight another day in a different setting.

How to organize

An effective enterprise ensures that collective effort is organized to achieve specific ends. Organizing involves dividing the overall management task into a variety of processes and activities and then establishing means of ensuring that these processes are carried out effectively and that the activities are coordinated. It is about differentiating activities in times of uncertainty and change, integrating them – grouping them together to achieve the organization's overall purpose – and ensuring that effective information flows and channels of communication are maintained.

Organization design

Organization design is based on the analysis of activities, processes, decisions, information flows and roles. It produces a structure that consists of positions and units between which there are relationships involving cooperation, the exercise of authority and the exchange of information.

Within the structure there will be line managers who are responsible for achieving results in the organization's key areas of activity by managing teams and individuals, and specialists who provide support, guidance and advice to the line.

The structure must be appropriate to the organization's purpose and technology, and the environment in which it exists. It must be flexible enough to adapt itself easily to new circumstances – organization design is a continuous process of modification and change; it is never a one-off event. It must also be recognized that, although the formal organization structure may define who is responsible for what and the ostensible lines of communication and control, the way in which it actually operates will depend on informal networks and other relationships that have not been defined in the design process and arise from people's daily interaction.

The approach to organization design

Organization design aims to clarify roles and relationships so far as this is possible in fluid conditions. It is also concerned with giving people the scope and opportunity to use their skills and abilities to better effect – this is the process of empowerment.

Jobs should be designed to satisfy the requirements of the organization for productivity, operational efficiency and quality of product or service. But they must also meet the needs of individuals for interest, challenge and accomplishment. These aims are interrelated and an important aim of organization and job design is to integrate the needs of the individual with those of the organization.

When it comes to designing or modifying the structure, a pragmatic approach is needed. It is first necessary to understand the environment, the technology and the existing systems of social relationships. An organization can then be designed that is contingent upon the circumstances. There is always some choice, but designers should try to achieve the best fit they can. And in making their choice, they should be aware of the structural, human, process and system factors that will influence the design, and of the context within which the organization operates.

Organization design is ultimately a matter of ensuring that the structure, processes and methods of operation fit the strategic requirements of the business and its technology within its environment. Disruption occurs if internal and external coherence and consistency are not achieved. And, as Mintzberg[1] suggests: 'Organizations, like individuals, can avoid identity crises by deciding what they wish to be and then pursuing it with a healthy obsession.'

Organization design is always an empirical and evolutionary process for which absolute principles cannot be laid down. But there are a number of broad guidelines that should be taken into account even if they are not followed slavishly.

Organization guidelines

Allocation of work

Related activities should be grouped logically together into functions and departments. Unnecessary overlap and duplication of work, either horizontally or vertically within a hierarchy, should be avoided.

A matrix organization may be developed in which multidisciplinary project teams are created specially to accomplish a specified task but the members of those teams are responsible on a continuing basis to a functional leader who allocates them to projects, assesses their performance, provides rewards and deals with training and career development needs.

Close attention should be given to the processes within the business. These are the interconnected sequences of activities that convert inputs into outputs. Thus, 'order fulfilment' is a process that starts with an order as its input and results in an 'output': the delivery of the ordered goods. The organization design should ensure that the flow of such processes can proceed smoothly, efficiently and effectively.

Business process re-engineering can help to achieve this by subjecting the processes that link key organizational functions together – from initiation to completion – to critical examination and, as necessary, redesign. It is sometimes better to organize these processes properly before becoming over-involved in the design of rigid structures that can inhibit the flow of work.

The work that needs to be done and accountabilities for results should be defined and agreed with teams and individual jobholders.

Matters requiring a decision should be dealt with as near to the point of action as possible by individuals or self-managing teams. Managers should not try to do too much themselves, nor should they supervise too closely.

Levels in the structure

Too many levels of management and supervision inhibit communication and teamwork and create extra work (and unnecessary jobs). The aim should be to reduce the number of levels to a minimum. However, the elimination of middle managers and wider spans of control mean that more attention has to be paid to improving teamwork, delegation and methods of integrating activities.

Span of control

There are limits to the number of people anyone can manage or supervise well, but these vary considerably between different jobs. Most people can work with a far greater span of control than they imagine, as long as they are prepared to delegate more effectively, to avoid becoming involved in too much detail, and to develop good teamwork among the individuals reporting to them. In fact, wide spans of control are beneficial in that they can enhance delegation and better teamwork and free the higher-level manager to spend more time on policy-making and planning.

Limited spans of control encourage managers to interfere too much with the work going on beneath them and therefore constrain the scope that should be given to their subordinates to grow with their jobs.

One person, one boss

Generally speaking, individuals should be accountable only to one boss for the results they achieve, to avoid confusion on operational matters. But in a project-based or matrix organization, individuals might be responsible to their project leader for contributing to the outcome of the project while also being responsible to their departmental manager or the head of their discipline for the continuing requirements of their role and for achieving agreed standards of overall performance.

Individuals in functional roles such as finance or personnel may be directly responsible to a line manager but may also have a 'dotted line' relationship of responsibility to the head of their function on matters of corporate policy.

Decentralization

Authority to make decisions should be delegated as close to the action as possible.

Optimize the structure

Develop an ideal organization by all means, but also remember that it may have to be modified to fit in the particular skills and abilities of key individuals.

Relevance to organizational needs

The organization has to be developed to meet the needs of its situation. In today's conditions of turbulence and change, this inevitably means a tendency towards more decentralized and flexible structures, with greater responsibility given to individuals and an extension of the use of task forces and project teams to deal with opportunities or threats. This implies an informal, non-bureaucratic, organic approach to organization design – the form of the organization will follow its function, not the other way around.

The organization may be largely based on multidisciplinary project teams, as in a matrix organization, or greater emphasis will be placed on ensuring that flows of work involved in the key business processes are properly catered for rather than the creation of a traditional formal and hierarchical structure.

The process of organization design

The process of organization design is to:

- define what the organization exists to do – its purpose and objectives;
- analyse and identify the processes, activities or tasks required to achieve those objectives and, as appropriate, the flow of decision-making and work throughout the organization;

- allocate related activities to teams and individual jobholders as appropriate;

- group related activities carried out by teams and individual jobholders logically into organizational units, while ensuring that the flow of work across organizational boundaries is not inhibited;

- provide for the management and coordination of the processes and activities at each level of responsibility;

- Ensure that attention is given to developing the processes of teamwork and communication;

- establish reporting and communicating relationships;

- recognize the importance of informal networks as means of communicating information and joint decision-making;

- provide, as far as possible, for organizational processes to adapt to change.

Defining structures

Structures are usually defined by means of organization charts. Such charts have their uses in planning and reviewing organizations. They can indicate how work is allocated and how activities are grouped together. They show who is responsible to whom, and they illustrate lines of authority. Drawing up a chart can be a good way of clarifying what is currently happening: the mere process of putting the organization down on paper will highlight any problems. And when it comes to considering changes, charts are the best way of illustrating alternatives.

The danger with organization charts is that they can be mistaken for the organization itself. They are no more than a snapshot of what is supposed to be happening at a given moment. They are out of date as soon as they are drawn, and they leave out the informal organization and its networks. If you use little boxes to represent people, they may behave as if they were indeed little boxes, sticking too closely to the rule book.

Charts can make people very conscious of their superiority or inferiority in relation to others. They can make it harder to change things, they can freeze relationships, and they can show relationships as they are supposed to be, not as they are. Robert Townsend[2] said of organization charts: 'Never formalize, print and circulate them. Good organizations are living bodies that grow new muscles to meet challenges.'

Defining roles

Role profiles, sometimes called role definitions, describe the part to be played by individuals in fulfilling their job requirements. They therefore indicate the behaviour required to carry out a particular task or the group of tasks contained in a job – they will set out the context within which individuals work as part of a team as well as the tasks they are expected to carry out.

The traditional form for defining roles is the job description, but, like organization charts, job descriptions can be too rigid and stifle initiative. It is better to use a role profile format along the following lines:

- role title;
- reporting relationships;
- main purpose of the role – a brief description of what the role exists to do;
- key result areas – the main areas of responsibility defined in terms of the results expected, without any attempt to go into any detail of how the work is done;
- competencies – the behavioural competencies required to carry out the role (behavioural competencies specify the types of behaviour required for successful performance of a role).

A role profile focuses on outcomes and behavioural requirements rather than tasks or duties. It does not prescribe in detail what has to be done.

Implementing structures

At the implementation stage it is necessary to ensure that everyone concerned:

- knows how they will be affected by the change;
- understands how their relationships with other people will change;
- accepts the reasons for the change and will not be reluctant to participate in its implementation.

It is easy to tell people what they are expected to do; it is much harder to get them to understand and accept how and why they should do it. The implementation plan should therefore cover not only the information to be given but also how it should be presented. The presentation will be easier if, in the analysis and design stage, full consultation has taken place with the individuals and groups who will be affected by the change. Too many organizational changes have failed because they have been imposed from above or from outside without proper consideration for the views and feelings of those most intimately concerned.

Implementation is often attempted by purely formal means – issuing edicts, distributing organization manuals or handing out job descriptions. These may be useful as far as they go, but while they provide information, they do not necessarily promote understanding and ownership. This can only be achieved on an informal but direct basis. Individuals must be given the opportunity to talk about what the proposed changes in their responsibilities will involve – they should already have been given the chance to contribute to the thinking behind the change, so discussions on the implications of the proposals should follow quite naturally. There is no guarantee that individuals who feel threatened by change will accept it, however much they have been consulted. But the attempt should be made. Departmental, team and inter-functional meetings can help to increase understanding. Change management is discussed in more detail in Chapter 16.

The implementation plan may have to cater for the likelihood that all the organizational changes cannot be implemented at once. Implementation may have to be phased to allow changes to be introduced progressively, to enable people to absorb what they will be expected to do and to allow for any necessary training. Changes may in any case be delayed until suitable people for new positions are available.

Endnotes

1 Mintzberg, H (1981) Organization design: fashion or fit, *Harvard Business Review*, January–February

2 Townsend, R (1970) *Up the Organization*, Michael Joseph, London

How to plan and prioritize   28

Planning

Planning is the process of deciding on a course of action, ensuring that the resources required to implement the action will be available and scheduling the programme of work required to achieve a defined end result. It also involves prioritizing work – deciding the order in which to do things.

As a manager, you will normally plan ahead over a relatively short period of time – up to one or, at most, two years. And your objectives, targets and budgets will probably have been fixed by the corporate plan or company budget.

You plan to complete tasks on time without using more resources than you were allowed. Your aim should be to avoid crises and the high costs that they cause, to have fewer 'drop everything and rush this' problems. Planning warns you about possible crises and gives you a chance to avoid them. Contingency or fall-back plans should be prepared if you have any reason to believe that your initial plan may fail for reasons beyond your control.

When you plan, you choose certain courses of action and rule out others; that is to say, you lose flexibility. This will be a disadvantage if the future turns out differently from what you expected – which is only too likely. Try to make plans that you can change at reasonable cost if you have to. It is a bad plan that admits no change.

Planning activities

As a manager, there are eight planning activities you need to carry out:

1 *Forecasting:*

- the sort of work that has to be done, how much and by when;
- how the workload might change;
- the likelihood of the department being called on to undertake specialized or rush jobs;
- possible changes within or outside the department that might affect priorities, the activities carried out, or the workload.

2 *Programming* – deciding the sequence and timescale of operations and events required to produce results on time.

3 *Staffing* – deciding how many and what type of staff are needed and considering the feasibility of absorbing peak loads by means of overtime or temporary staff.

4 *Setting standards and targets* – for output, sales, times, quality, costs or for any other aspect of the work where performance should be planned, measured and controlled.

5 *Procedure planning* – deciding how the work should be done and planning the actual operations by defining the systems and procedures required.

6 *Materials planning* – deciding what materials, bought-in parts or subcontracted work are required and ensuring that they are made available in the right quantity at the right time.

7 *Facilities planning* – deciding on the plant, equipment, tools and space required.

8 *Budgeting* – ensuring that the financial resources required will be available, preparing financial budgets and controlling expenditures.

Planning techniques

Most of the planning you do as a manager is simply a matter of thinking systematically and using your common sense. Every plan contains three key ingredients:

1 *Objective* – the innovation or improvement to be achieved.

2 *Action programme* – the specific steps required to achieve the right objective.

3 *Financial impact* – the effect of the action on sales, turnover, costs and, ultimately, profit.

Table 28.1 is an example of how a manufacturing plan could be set out.

Bar charts can be used to express plans more graphically wherever there is more than one activity and care has to be taken to sequence them correctly. The manufacturing plan illustrated in Table 28.1 could be expressed as a Gantt chart (see Figure 28.1).

Table 28.1 A manufacturing plan

Steps	Responsibility	Completion by
1 Ensure recognition by supplier of 'hard spots' in castings.	Supplies Manager	15 January
2 Negotiate price concessions on all castings received during weeks when we return more than 10 bad castings.	Supplies Manager	31 January
3 Set up storage area to store defective castings.	Facilities Manager	15 February
4 Establish procedures to record machine downtime and cutter breakdown with individual castings.	Production Controller	1 March
5 Ensure supplier agrees new arrangements.	Supplies Manager	15 March

Figure 28.1   A Gantt chart

Step (detailed in action programme)	Responsibility	January	February	March
1 Get supplier to recognize problem	Supplies Manager	▬		
2 Negotiate price concession	Supplies Manager		▬	
3 Set up storage area	Facilities Manager		▬	
4 Establish new recording procedures	Production Controller			▬
5 Ensure supplier agrees new arrangements	Supplies Manager			▬

A more refined method of planning activities in a complex programme, where many interdependent events have to take place, is network planning. This requires the recording of the component parts and their representation in a diagram as a network of inter-related activities. Events are represented by circles, activities by arrows, and the time taken by activities by the length of the arrows. There can also be dotted arrows for dummy activities between events that have a time rather than an activity relationship. A critical path can be derived that highlights those operations or activities that are essential for the completion of the project within the allocated timescale. An illustration of part of a basic network is given in Figure 28.2.

There may be occasions when even more sophisticated planning techniques, using computer models, can be made available to help the manager, especially when large quantities of information have

Figure 28.2 Part of a basic network

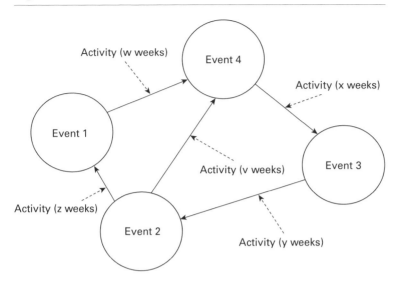

to be processed against a number of fixed assumptions or parameters, or where alternative assumptions have to be assessed. Plans can then be made to ensure that workers and machine capacity are available to deal with forecast work levels.

How to prioritize

Planning involves prioritizing work, which means deciding on the relative importance of a range of demands or tasks so that the order in which they are undertaken can be determined. The fragmented nature of managerial work and the sudden and often conflicting demands made on your time mean that you will constantly be faced with decisions on when to do things. There may often be situations when you have to cope with conflicting priorities. This can be stressful unless you adopt a systematic approach to prioritization.

Prioritization can be carried out in the following stages:

1 List all the things you have to do. These can be classified into three groups:

- regular duties such as submitting a report, calling on customers, carrying out a performance review;

- special requests from managers, colleagues, customers, clients, suppliers and so on, delivered orally, by e-mail, telephone, letter, or fax;

- self-generated work such as preparing proposals on a new procedure.

2 Classify each item on the list according to:

- the significance of the task to be done in terms of its impact on your work (and reputation) and on the results achieved by the organization, your team or anyone else involved;

- the importance of the person requesting the work or expecting you to deliver something – less significant tasks may well be put higher on the priority list if they are set by the chief executive or a key client;

- the urgency of the tasks – deadlines, what will happen if they are not completed on time;

- any scope there may be for extending deadlines – altering start and finish times and dates;

- how long each task will take to complete – noting any required or imposed starting and completion times that cannot be changed.

Assess how much time you have available to complete the tasks, apart from the routine work that you must get done. Also assess what resources, such as your own staff, are available to get the work done.

3 Draw up a provisional list of priorities by reference to the criteria of significance, importance and urgency listed at (2) above.

4 Assess the possibility of fitting this prioritized schedule of work into the time available. If this proves difficult, put self-imposed priorities on a back burner and concentrate on the significant tasks. Negotiate delayed completion or delivery times where you believe this is possible, and if successful, move the task down the priority list.

5 Finalize the list of priorities and schedule the work you have to do (or you have to get others to do) accordingly.

Set out step by step like this, prioritization looks like a formidable task. But experienced managers go through all these stages almost unconsciously, although systematically, whenever they are confronted with a large workload or conflicting priorities.

What many people do is simply write out a 'things to do' list at the beginning of the week or, in their mind, quickly run through all the considerations described in the above six-stage sequence and make notes on the order in which they should be tackled.

How to deal with office politics

29

Office politics – good or bad?

To be politic, according to the *Oxford English Dictionary*, you can be sagacious, prudent, judicious, expedient, scheming or crafty. So political behaviour in an organization could be desirable or undesirable.

Organizations consist of individuals who, while they are ostensibly there to achieve a common purpose, will, at the same time, be driven by their own needs to achieve their own goals. Effective management is the process of harmonizing individual endeavour and ambition to the common good. Some individuals will genuinely believe that using political means to achieve their goals will benefit the organization as well as themselves. Others will rationalize this belief. Yet others will unashamedly pursue their own ends. They may use all their powers of persuasion to legitimize these ends to their colleagues, but self-interest remains their primary drive. These are the corporate politicians, whom the *Oxford English Dictionary* describes as 'shrewd schemers, crafty plotters or intriguers'. Politicians within organizations can be like this. They manoeuvre behind people's backs, blocking proposals they do not like. They advance their own reputation and career at the expense of other people. They can be envious and jealous and act accordingly. They are bad news.

But it can also be argued that a political approach to management is inevitable and even desirable in any organization where the clarity of goals is not absolute, where the decision-making process is not clear-cut and where the authority to make decisions is not evenly or appropriately distributed. And there can be few organizations where one or more of these conditions do not apply.

Andrew Kakabadse[1] recognizes this point when he says in *The Politics of Management*: 'Politics is a process, that of influencing individuals and groups of people to your point of view, where you cannot rely on authority.' In this sense, a political approach can be legitimate as long as the ends are justifiable from the viewpoint of the organization.

Political approaches

Kakabadse identifies seven approaches that office politicians adopt:

1 Identify the stakeholders, those who have commitment to act in a particular way.

2 Keep the stakeholders comfortable, concentrating on behaviour, values, attitudes, fears and drives that the individuals will accept, tolerate and manage (comfort zones).

3 Fit the image – work on the comfort zones and align their image to that of the people with power.

4 Use the network – identify the interest groups and people of influence.

5 Enter the network – identify the gatekeepers, adhere to the norms.

6 Make deals – agree to support other people where this is of mutual benefit.

7 Withhold and withdraw – withhold information as appropriate and withdraw judiciously when the going gets rough.

Some of these precepts are more legitimate than others. Organizational life requires managers to identify the key decision-makers when they are involved in developing new approaches and getting things done. Before coming to a final conclusion and launching a fully fledged proposal at a committee or in a memorandum, it makes good sense to test opinion and find out how other people may react. This testing process enables managers to anticipate counter-arguments and modify their proposals either to meet legitimate objections or, when there is no alternative, to accommodate other people's requirements.

Making deals may not appear to be particularly desirable but it does happen, and managers can always rationalize this type of behaviour by reference to the end result. Withholding information is not legitimate behaviour, but people do indulge in it in recognition of the fact that knowledge is power. Judicious withdrawal may also seem to be questionable, but most managers prefer to live to fight another day rather than launch a doomed crusade.

Political sensitivity

Office politicians exert hidden influence to get their way, and 'politicking' in some form takes place in most organizations. If you want to get on, a degree of political sensitivity – knowing what is going on so that influence can be exerted – is desirable. This means:

- knowing how 'things are done around here';
- knowing how decisions are made, including the less obvious factors that are likely to affect decisions;
- knowing where the power base is in the organization – who makes the running; who are the people who count when decisions are taken;
- being aware of what is going on behind the scenes;
- knowing who is a rising star and whose reputation is fading;
- identifying any 'hidden agendas' – trying to understand what people are really getting at, and why, by obtaining answers to the question: 'Where are they coming from?'
- finding out what other people are thinking and seeking;
- networking – as Kakabadse suggests, identifying the interest groups.

Dangers

The danger of politics, however, is that it can be carried to excess, and can then seriously harm the effectiveness of an organization. The signs of excessive indulgence in political behaviour include:

- back-biting;
- buck-passing;
- secret meetings and hidden decisions;
- feuds between people and departments;
- paper or e-mail wars between armed camps – arguing by memoranda or e-mail, always a sign of distrust;
- a multiplicity of snide comments and criticisms;
- excessive and counterproductive lobbying;
- the formation of cabals – cliques that spend their time intriguing.

Dealing with office politicians

One way to deal with this sort of behaviour is to find out who is going in for it and openly confront them with the damage they are doing. They will, of course, deny that they are behaving politically (they wouldn't be politicians if they didn't), but the fact that they have been identified might lead them to modify their approach. It could, of course, only serve to drive them further underground, in which case their behaviour will have to be observed even more closely and corrective action taken as necessary.

A more positive approach to keeping politics operating at an acceptable level is for the organization to manage its operations as openly as possible. The aims should be to ensure that issues are debated fully, that differences of opinion are dealt with frankly and that disagreements are depersonalized, so far as this is possible. Political processes can then be seen as a way of maintaining the momentum of the organization as a complex decision-making and problem-solving entity.

Use of politics

There are occasions when a subtle appeal rather than a direct attack will pay dividends, and sometimes you have to exercise your powers of persuasion indirectly on those whose support your need. The following case study illustrates the legitimate use of politics.

CASE STUDY

James Hale was the personnel director of a large divisionalized group in the food industry. The rate of growth by expansion and acquisitions had been very rapid. There was a shortage of really good managers and a lack of coordination between the divisions in the group and between those divisions and head office. Hale believed that setting up a group management training centre would be a good way of helping to overcome these problems. He knew, however, that he would have to get agreement to this plan not only from the managing director, who would be broadly sympathetic, but also from his co-directors. The MD would not act without the support of a majority on his board. In any case, Hale genuinely felt that there was no point in developing a facility of this sort for people who were not interested in it.

He therefore sat back and deliberately worked out a strategy for getting agreement to his proposal. He knew that a frontal attack might fail. Management development was perceived by his colleagues as a somewhat airy-fairy idea that had little relevance to their real concerns as directors. He therefore had to adopt a more subtle approach. He did not call it a political campaign, but that is what it was. He was setting out to influence people indirectly.

The basis of his plan was an individual approach to each of his colleagues, adjusted to their particular interests and concerns. In the case of the marketing director, he got the general sales manager to advocate the need for training in sales management for divisional sales staff. He ran several pilot courses in hotels and invited the marketing director to the winding-up session. He made sure that the marketing director was impressed not only by what the divisional sales staff had learnt from the course, but also by the new spirit of identification with group aims and policies engendered by the training. Casually, the personnel director let slip the thought that if the group had its own training centre this feeling of commitment could be developed even more strongly.

The same basic technique was used with the production director, who was nudged towards the view that a centre owned by the group could speed up the introduction of new ideas and provide a facility for communicating directly with key staff that was not available at present.

The finance director was a more difficult person to convince. He could easily assess the costs but found it difficult to accept largely subjective views of the potential benefits. In this case, James Hale did not try too hard to persuade him against his will. He knew that the majority of the board, including the managing director, were now in favour of the plan. Hale felt safe in leaving his financial colleague in an isolated and ultimately untenable position. The qualitative arguments, as absorbed by the other members of the board, had the ring of truth about them that no purely quantitative arguments could overcome.

Hale was content that he had enough support. To clinch the argument, he played his last political card by warning the marketing and production directors that there might be some financial opposition.

He then got them to agree with the thesis that they wouldn't allow 'Mr Money Bags' to adopt a narrow financial view and thus dictate the destiny of the firm.

James Hale had no difficulty in getting his proposal accepted at the next board meeting.

The non-legitimate use of politics

The following is an example of non-legitimate use of politics. Unfortunately, it is a fairly common one. In most organizations there are people who want to get on, and do not have too many scruples about how they do it. If it involves treading on other people's faces, then so be it.

CASE STUDY

Two directors of a company both aspired to be the next managing director. Mr Gray, the finance director, had the ear of the MD. Mr White, the technical director, was more remote.

Mr White had a number of ideas for introducing new technology and had proved, to his own satisfaction at least, that the pay-off was considerable. Unfortunately, he jumped the gun in order to anticipate comments from Gray, and presented a paper to the managing director that was not as well argued as it might have been. Gray carefully lobbied the MD and convinced him that the proposal was full of holes – he also hinted that this was yet another example of White's inability to understand the wider commercial issues.

The MD accepted this view more or less completely and agreed with Gray's suggestion that the whole proposal should be off-loaded on to a board sub-committee – a well-known device to delay if not to stifle new ideas. This was done, and the introduction of new technology was unnecessarily delayed by 18 months. But Gray had made his point as the practical man of affairs who would not allow the company to get involved in expensive and unrewarding projects.

Endnote

1 Kakabadse, A (1983) *The Politics of Management*, Gower, Aldershot

PART FOUR
Personal skills

How to assess your own performance

30

To be a better manager you need to understand how well you are performing – your strengths and weaknesses. This will provide the basis for self-development as discussed in Chapter 31.

Peter Drucker[1] proposed that: 'The only way to discover your strengths is through feedback analysis. Whenever you make a key decision or take a key action, write down what you expect will happen. Nine or twelve months later, compare the actual results with your expectations.'

But it is also helpful to make a general assessment of your strengths and weaknesses and conduct an overall review of how you do your job as described below.

Self-assessment questionnaire

Table 30.1 Self-assessment questionnaire

I think I am someone who is:	Strongly agree	Agree	Neither agree nor disagree	Disagree	Strongly disagree
Outgoing, likes people					
Emotionally stable					
Easily upset					

(continued)

Table 30.1 (*Continued*)

I think I am someone who is:	Strongly agree	Agree	Neither agree nor disagree	Disagree	Strongly disagree
Forceful, domineering					
Cooperative, accommodating					
Lively, enthusiastic					
Serious, introspective					
Imaginative, creative					
Prosaic, conventional					
Astute, diplomatic					
Self-assured, confident					
Open to change					
Traditional					
Self-reliant, individualistic					
Group orientated, a joiner					
Driven					
Relaxed					

Job performance review

You should examine your job and how you do it as follows:

1 Ensure that you are clear about what your job entails in terms of its key result areas – the most important things you are expected to do. If in doubt, ask your manager for clarification.

2 Find out what you are expected to achieve for each of the key result areas. Expectations should be definable as objectives in the form of quantified targets or standards of performance (qualitative statements of what constitutes effective performance). Ideally they should have been discussed and agreed as part of the performance appraisal/management process but if this has not happened, ask your manager to spell out what he or she expects you to achieve.

3 Refer to the organization's competency framework. Discuss with your manager how he or she interprets these as far as you are concerned.

4 At fairly regular intervals, say once a month, review your progress by reference to the objectives, standards and competency headings. Take note of your achievements and, if they exist, your failures. Analyse your strengths and weaknesses. Ask yourself why you were successful or unsuccessful and what you can do to build on success or overcome failure. You may identify actions you can take or specific changes in behaviour you can try to achieve. Or you may identify a need for further coaching, training or experience.

5 At the end of the review period and prior to the appraisal discussion with your manager, look back at each of your interim reviews and the actions you decided to take. Consider what more needs to be done in any specific area or generally. You will then be in a position to answer the following questions that might be posed by your manager before or during the appraisal discussion:

- How do you feel you have done?
- What are you best at doing?
- Are there any parts of your job which you find difficult?
- Are there any aspects of your work in which you would benefit from better guidance or further training?

Endnote

1 Drucker, P (1999) Managing oneself, *Harvard Business Review*, March/April, pp 66–74

How to get on   31

Getting on is first about knowing who you are and what you can do – your strengths and weaknesses as described in Chapter 30.

Beyond that there are certain actions you can take that will help you to get on. Some are obvious, others less so. How you apply them will depend on your assessment of where you are and what you can do. The main things to do, as described below, are to:

- know what you want;
- display the personal qualities and behave in the ways that will contribute to your success;
- take steps to develop yourself.

Know what you want

Knowing what you want is the key to getting on. There are eight things to do:

1 Decide what you want to do and then go for it. Believe that if you really want something you can get it, and act accordingly.

2 Set demanding targets and deadlines for yourself. 'People grow according to the demands they make on themselves' (Drucker[1]). But don't over-commit yourself. Be realistic about what you can achieve.

3 Pursue excellence. 'If you can't do it excellently don't do it at all' (Townsend[2]).

4 Focus on what you can contribute. 'To ask "what can I contribute?" is to look for the unused potential in a job' (Drucker[1]).

5 Get your priorities right. Adapt Drucker's rules for identifying them:

- pick the future as against the past;
- focus on opportunities rather than on problems;
- choose your own direction – rather than climb on the bandwagon;
- aim high, aim for something that will make a difference rather than something that is 'safe' and easy to do.

6 Keep it simple. Concentrate. Consider all your tasks and eliminate the irrelevant ones. Slough off old activities before you start new ones. 'Concentration is the key to economic results... no other principle of effectiveness is violated as constantly today as the basic principle of concentration... Our motto seems to be: "let's do a little bit of everything"' (Drucker[1]).

7 Take the broad view but don't ignore the significant detail: 'Ill can he rule the great, that cannot reach the small' (Edmund Spenser). It is sometimes necessary to penetrate beneath the surface to find out what is really happening – on the shop floor or in the field. But do this selectively.

8 Adapt to changing demands. 'The executive who keeps on doing what he has done successfully before is almost bound to fail' (Drucker[1]).

Personal qualities and behaviour

1 Be enthusiastic and show it.

2 Innovate and create – come up with new ideas and react positively to other people's ideas. Don't sulk if your ideas are not accepted. Try again another way.

3 Show willing – there is nothing worse than the person who always moans when he is given something to do. Don't say: 'How can I possibly do that?' Instead, respond immediately with something like this: 'Right, this is what I propose to do – is that what you want?'

4 Be positive – in the words of the old Bing Crosby song: 'accentuate the positive, eliminate the negative.'

5 Work hard – people who get on are hard workers. But they don't work for work's sake. Effectiveness is never a function of how late you stay in the office. It's what you do while you are there that counts.

6 Present yourself well – life is not all about making a good impression, but you might as well make sure that your achievements are known and appreciated. And if people are impressed by executives who are decisive, punctual and answer promptly, why not impress them that way? More good than harm will come of it.

7 Be ambitious – 'A man's reach should exceed his grasp, or what's a heaven for?' (Robert Browning). But don't overdo it. Don't appear to be more concerned about your future status than about present effectiveness.

8 Be courageous – take calculated risks, believe in what you are doing and stick to your guns.

9 Be assertive but not aggressive.

10 Put your points across firmly and succinctly.

11 Don't talk too much. Never over-commit yourself. Save up what you want to say until the right moment. Keep your powder dry. Don't shoot your mouth off. 'Whereof one cannot speak, thereon one must remain silent' (Wittgenstein).

12 Learn to cope with stress. You won't avoid it and you have to live with it. If problems are coming at you thick and fast, try to slow down. Relax. Take a little time off. Give yourself a chance to put the situation into perspective.

13 If things go wrong, bounce back. Accept reverses calmly. Think about what you need to do and then get into action – fast. There is nothing like purposeful activity in these circumstances.

14 Get people to trust you – you will do this if you never lie or even shade the truth, if you avoid playing politics and if you always deliver what you promise.

15 Accept constructive criticism.

16 'Admit your own mistakes openly, even joyfully' (Townsend[2]). Never make an excuse. Accept the responsibility and the blame if you make a mistake.

17 Consider the extent to which you display emotional intelligence in carrying out your work, and do something about it if you are lacking in this essential requirement, as described in Chapter 32.

Develop yourself

The best way to get on is to rely on yourself, while seeking and benefiting from any support you can get from your manager or the organization. Self-development takes place through self-managed or self-directed learning. This means that you take responsibility for satisfying your own learning needs to improve performance, to support the achievement of career aspirations, or to enhance your experience within and beyond your present organization. It can be based on processes that enable you to identify what you need to learn, by reflecting on your experience and analysing what you need to know and be able to do, so that you can perform better and progress your career.

The case for self-managed learning is that people learn and retain more if they find things out for themselves. But they may still need to be helped to identify what they should look for. Self-managed learning is about self-development, and this will be furthered by self-assessment, which leads to better self-understanding.

Michael Pedler and his colleagues[3] recommend the following four-stage approach:

1 self-assessment based on analysis by individuals of their work and life situation;

2 diagnosis derived from the analysis of learning needs and priorities;

3 action planning to identify objectives, helps and hindrances, resources required (including people) and timescales;

4 monitoring and review to assess progress in achieving action plans.

Identify development needs

You can use performance management processes as described in Chapter 6 to identify self-development needs on your own or in discussion with your boss. This will include reviewing performance against agreed plans, and assessing competence requirements and your capacity to achieve them. The analysis is therefore based on an understanding of what you are expected to do, the knowledge and skills you need to carry out your job effectively, what you have achieved, and what knowledge and skills you have. If there are any gaps between the knowledge and skills you need and those you have, then this defines a development need. The analysis is always related to work and the capacity to carry it out effectively.

By making your own assessment of your personal development needs a basis for identifying the means of satisfying them and acting accordingly, you can get more satisfaction from your work, advance your career and increase your employability.

Define the means of satisfying development needs

When deciding how to satisfy the needs you should remember that it is not just about selecting suitable training courses. These may form part of your development plan, but only a minor part; other learning activities are much more important. Examples of development activities include: observing and analysing what others do (good practice); planned use of internal training media, including e-learning (use of electronic learning materials) and learning libraries; being coached; training courses; distance learning – learning in your own time from material prepared elsewhere, such as correspondence courses; guided reading; project work or special assignments; working with a mentor; involvement in other work areas; input to policy formulation; increased professionalism on the job; involvement in the community; coaching others.

Personal development plans

A personal development plan sets out the actions you propose to take to learn and to develop yourself. You take responsibility for formulating and implementing the plan, but you may receive support from the organization and your manager in doing so.

Personal development planning aims to promote learning and to provide you with knowledge and a portfolio of transferable skills that will help to progress your career.

A personal development action plan sets out what needs to be done and how it will be done under headings such as:

● development needs;

● outcomes expected (learning objectives);

● development activities to meet the needs;

● responsibility for development – what individuals will do and what support they will require from their manager, the HR department or other people;

● timing – when the learning activity is expected to start and be completed;

● outcome – what development activities have taken place and how effective they were.

10 self-development steps

The following are 10 steps you can take to develop yourself:

1 *Create a development log* – record your plans and action.

2 *State your objectives* – the career path you want to follow and the skills you will need to proceed along that path.

3 *Develop a personal profile* – what sort of person you are, your likes and dislikes about work, your aspirations.

4 *List your strengths and weaknesses.*

5 *List your achievements* – what you have done well so far and why you believe these were worthwhile achievements.

6 *List significant learning experiences* – recall events when you have learnt something worthwhile (this can help you to understand your learning style).

7 *Ask other people* about your strengths and weaknesses and what you should do to develop yourself.

8 *Focus on the present* – what is happening to you now: your job, your current skills, your short-term development needs.

9 *Focus on the future* – where you want to be in the longer term and how you are going to get there (including a list of the skills and abilities you need to develop).

10 *Plan your self-development strategy* – how you are going to achieve your ambitions.

Endnotes

1 Drucker, P (1955) *The Practice of Management*, Heinemann, London

2 Townsend, R (1970) *Up the Organization*, Michael Joseph, London

3 Pedler, M, Burgoyne J and Boydell, T (1994) *A Manager's Guide to Self-Development*, McGraw-Hill, Maidenhead

How to develop 32 your emotional intelligence

The significance of emotional intelligence

To succeed it is not enough to have technical ability and a high IQ (intelligence quotient); emotional intelligence is also required. It is a familiar situation. Someone with lots of technical, professional or specialist expertise is promoted to a managerial job and fails. This may be partly attributed to an inability to manage in the sense of planning, organizing and controlling the use of resources. But the main reason is probably a failure to manage personal relationships as a leader or a colleague, and this may be attributed the individual's lack of understanding of their own emotions and an inability to appreciate the emotions of people with whom he or she is involved. In other words, an inadequate level of emotional intelligence.

The components of emotional intelligence

The four components of emotional intelligence identified by Daniel Goleman[1] are:

1 *Self-management* – the ability to control or redirect disruptive impulses and moods and regulate one's own behaviour, coupled

with a propensity to pursue goals with energy and persistence. The six competencies associated with this component are self-control, trustworthiness and integrity, initiative, adaptability – comfort with ambiguity – openness to change and strong desire to achieve.

2 *Self-awareness* – the ability to recognize and understand your moods, emotions and drives as well as their effect on others. This is linked to three competencies: self-confidence, realistic self-assessment and emotional self-awareness.

3 *Social awareness* – the ability to understand the emotional make-up of other people and skill in treating people according to their emotional reactions. This is linked to six competencies: empathy, expertise in building and retaining talent, organizational awareness, cross-cultural sensitivity, valuing diversity and service to clients and customers.

4 *Social skills* – proficiency in managing relationships and building networks to get the desired result from others and reach personal goals, and the ability to find common ground and build rapport. The five competencies associated with this component are: leadership, effectiveness in leading change, conflict management, influence/communication and expertise in building and leading teams.

Developing emotional intelligence

What organizations do

When organizations try to help people develop their emotional intelligence they take the following steps:

1 Assess the requirements of jobs in terms of emotional skills.

2 Assess individuals to identify their level of emotional intelligence – 360-degree feedback (ie getting feedback from colleagues, clients or customers and subordinates as well as one's boss) can be a powerful source of data; instruments such as the Bar-on Emotional Quotient Inventory can be used to measure levels of emotional intelligence.

3   Gauge readiness – ensure that people are prepared to improve their level of emotional intelligence.

4   Motivate people to believe that the learning experience will benefit them.

5   Make change self-directed – encourage people to prepare a learning plan that fits their interests, resources and goals.

6   Focus on clear manageable goals – the focus must be on immediate, manageable steps, bearing in mind that cultivating a new skill is gradual.

7   Prevent relapse – show people how they can learn lessons from the inevitable relapses.

8   Give performance feedback.

9   Encourage practice, remembering that emotional competence cannot be improved overnight.

10   Provide models of desired behaviours.

11   Encourage and reinforce – create a climate that rewards self-improvement.

12   Evaluate – establish sound outcome measures and then assess performance against them.

What you can do

Your organization can do much to help. But there is a lot you can do for yourself. Allowing for the nature of emotional intelligence, the following are 10 steps you can take:

1   Recognize that only you can improve the results you achieve.

2   Get to know yourself better by carrying out a formal self-assessment using the approach described in Chapter 30. Obtain answers to questions such as: 'What aspects of my performance are going well?', 'What aspects of my performance do I need to improve?' and 'What do I need to do to improve my emotional intelligence skills (interacting with other people)?'

3 On the basis of this assessment, take Goleman's four components of emotional intelligence listed above, and analyse your own behaviour and the impact it has made on other people. Obtain answers to the following questions: 'How good am I at self-management?', 'How self-aware am I?', 'How socially aware am I?' and 'How effective are my social skills?'

4 Seek feedback from your boss, your colleagues, your subordinates and your clients. Try to find out what impression you make on them and where they think you could do better.

5 Focus on those aspects of your behaviour where, first, there is the most room for improvement, and second, the likelihood of being able to change is reasonably high. Don't expect quick results. Changing behaviour can be a long haul.

6 Refer to specific aspects of behaviour rather than generalizations.

7 If possible, get help from a mentor, a counsellor or an executive coach. The latter can be particularly useful if they know their job.

8 Make the most of any training or development courses your organization provides on such matters as leadership, teamwork and interpersonal skills.

9 Use your imagination and be patient. You will not necessarily get easy answers to your quest for improvements. You will not change ingrained behavioural habits without being quite radical in your approach. And you have to recognize that it will take time.

10 Monitor progress by analysing your own behaviour and the impact it makes, and obtaining further feedback from others. Adjust your development programme as necessary in the light of this feedback.

Endnote

1 Goleman, D (2000) Leadership that gets results, *Harvard Business Review*, March/April, pp 78–90

How to be confident

33

To be confident is to be self-assured with a firm belief in one's capacity to get things done well. Confidence was defined by Rob Yeung as 'the ability take appropriate and effective action, however challenging it may appear at the time'.

Confident people are positive about what they do and optimistic about their ability to deal with the situations they face. As David Preston[2] explains: 'Confident people believe they can be whatever they want to be and accomplish anything they choose.'

He also pointed out that confidence is based on:

- self-worth – the value you place on yourself;
- competence – your beliefs about your capacity to achieve;
- belonging – whether you feel accepted and respected by others.

Confidence is learned. It develops during childhood and formal education and at work and in adult life. Positive experiences create confidence, negative ones can undermine it and need to be dealt with. As David Preston points out, 'Anything which has been learned can be reappraised and replaced with new, superior learning.' He also noted that: 'When you speak and act confidently others treat you accordingly, which reinforces your behaviour and makes you feel even more confident.'

Developing confidence – 12 steps

1 Focus on what you can do well, not your limitations.

2 Act confidently (even if you feel underconfident) so that people believe that you *are* confident. Their belief will reinforce your self-belief.

3 Convey your confidence to others by speaking out and varying the pace, pitch and emphasis of your voice. Look them in the eye (but don't try to stare them out).

4 Focus on the present. Don't dwell on the past or worry about the future.

5 Find out what works for you, how it works and when it works.

6 Recognize and celebrate your achievements.

7 Cultivate resilience. Bounce back from setbacks. As Browning wrote: 'Dry your eyes and laugh at a fall and quickly get up to begin again.'

8 Develop self-belief. If you believe you can do something you will do it. If you don't you won't.

9 Understand the challenges you will face and, based on your experience, how you will overcome them.

10 Set yourself goals and work on how to achieve them.

11 As David Preston proposed, say to yourself: 'I've done it before I can do it again.'

12 Analyse how confident people behave.

Endnotes

1 Yeung, Rob (2011) *Confidence*, Prentice Hall Life, Harlow

2 Preston, David L (2010) *365 Steps to Self-confidence*, Howtobooks, Oxford

How to be assertive

34

Assertion and aggression

Assertiveness is:

- standing up for your own rights in such a way that you do not violate another person's rights;
- expressing your needs, wants, opinions, feelings and beliefs in direct, honest and appropriate ways.

When you are being assertive you are not, therefore, being aggressive, which means violating or ignoring other people's rights in order to get your own way or dominate a situation.

Aggressive behaviour causes one of two counterproductive reactions: fight or flight. In other words, aggression either breeds aggression, which gets you nowhere, or it forces people to retreat in a demoralized or dissatisfied way. Indulging in this sort of behaviour will not help to achieve your aim of getting them to go along with you.

Assertive behaviour

Behaving assertively puts you into the position of being able to influence people properly and react to them positively. Assertive statements:

- are brief and to the point;
- indicate clearly that you are not hiding behind something or someone and are speaking for yourself by using words such as: 'I think that...', 'I believe that...', 'I feel that...';

- are not overweighted with advice;
- use questions to find out the views of others and to test their reactions to your behaviour;
- distinguish between fact and opinion;
- are expressed positively but not dogmatically;
- indicate that you are aware that the other people have different points of view;
- express, when necessary, negative feelings about the effects of other people's behaviour on you – pointing out in dispassionate and factual terms the feelings aroused in you by that behaviour, and suggesting the behaviour you would prefer;
- point out to people politely but firmly the consequences of their behaviour.

Handling aggression

If you are faced by aggression, take a breath, count up to 10 and then:

- Ask calmly for information about what is bugging the aggressors.
- State clearly, and again calmly, the position as you see it.
- Empathize with the aggressors by making it plain that you can see it from their point of view, but at the same time explaining in a matter-of-fact way how you see the discrepancy between what they believe and what you feel is actually happening.
- Indicate, if the aggressive behaviour persists, your different beliefs or feelings, but do not cut aggressors short – people often talk, or even shout, themselves out of being aggressive when they realize that you are not reacting aggressively and that their behaviour is not getting them anywhere.
- Suggest, if all else fails, that you leave it for the time being and talk about it again after a cooling-off period.

Influencing styles

Assertiveness is about fighting your own corner. You have to believe in yourself and what you are doing and express these beliefs confidently and without hesitation. It is about using influencing skills.

There are four influencing styles you can use:

1 *Asserting* – making your views clear.

2 *Persuading* – using facts, logic and reason to present your own case, emphasizing its strong points (benefits to the organization or the individual(s) you are dealing with), anticipating objections to any apparent weaknesses and appealing to reason.

3 *Bridging* – drawing out other people's points of view, demonstrating that you understand what they are getting at, giving credit and praise in response to their good ideas and suggestions, joining your views with theirs.

4 *Attracting* – conveying your enthusiasm for your ideas, making people feel that they are all part of an exciting project.

There is more about influencing people in Chapter 23.

How to be decisive

35

Good managers are decisive. They can quickly size up a situation and reach the right conclusion on what should be done about it.

To say someone 'is decisive' is praise indeed as long as it is understood that the decisions are effective. To be decisive it is first necessary to know something about the decision-making process as summarized below. You should also be familiar with the techniques of problem-solving, as explained in the next chapter. Armed with this knowledge you can adopt the approaches described at the end of this chapter.

Characteristics of the decision-making process

Decision-making is about analysing a situation or problem, identifying possible courses of action, weighing them up and defining the preferred action.

Peter Drucker[1] says:

> A decision is a judgement. It is a choice between alternatives. It is rarely a choice between right and wrong. It is at best a choice between almost right and probably wrong – but much more often a choice between two courses of action, neither of which is probably more nearly right than the other.

You should not expect or even welcome a bland consensus view. The best decisions emerge from conflicting viewpoints. This is Drucker's first law of decision-making: 'One does not make a decision without disagreements.' You can benefit from a clash of opinion to prevent people falling into the trap of starting with the conclusion and then looking for the facts that support it.

Alfred P Sloan of General Motors knew this. At a meeting of one of his top committees he said, 'Gentlemen, I take it we are all in agreement on the decision here.' Everyone around the table nodded assent. 'Then', continued Mr Sloan, 'I propose we postpone further discussion of the matter until our next meeting to give ourselves time to develop disagreement and perhaps gain some understanding of what the decision is all about.'

10 approaches to being decisive

1   *Make decisions faster* – Jack Welch, when heading General Electric, used to say: 'In today's lightning-paced environment, you don't have time to think about things. Don't sit on decisions. Empty that in-basket so that you are free to search out new opportunities... Don't sit still. Anybody sitting still, you are going to guarantee they're going to get their legs knocked from under them.'

2   *Avoid procrastination* – it is easy to put an e-mail demanding a decision into the 'too difficult' section of your actual or mental in-tray. Avoid the temptation to fill your time with trivial tasks so that the evil moment when you have to address the issue is postponed. Make a start. Once you have got going you can deal with the unpleasant task of making a decision in stages. A challenge often becomes easier once we have started dealing with it. Having spent five minutes on it we don't want to feel it was time wasted, so we carry on and complete the job.

3   *Expect the unexpected* – you are then in the frame of mind needed to respond decisively to a new situation.

4   *Think before you act* – this could be a recipe for delay, but decisive people use their analytical ability to come to swift conclusions about the nature of the situation and what should be done about it.

5 *Be careful about assumptions* – we have a tendency to leap to conclusions and seize on assumptions that support our case and ignore the facts that might contradict it.

6 *Learn from the past* – build on your experience in decision-making; what approaches work best. But don't rely too much on precedents. Situations change. The right decision last time could well be the wrong one now.

7 *Be systematic* – adopt a rigorous problem-solving approach as described in Chapter 36. This means specifying objectives – what you want to achieve – defining the criteria for judging whether they have been achieved, getting and analysing the facts, looking for causes rather than focusing on symptoms, developing and testing hypotheses and alternative solutions, and evaluating possible causes of action against the objectives and criteria.

8 *Talk it through* – before you make a significant decision talk it through with someone who is likely to disagree so that any challenge they make can be taken into account (but you have to canvass opinion swiftly).

9 *Leave time to think it over* – swift decision-making is highly desirable but you must avoid knee-jerk reactions. Pause, if only for a few minutes, to allow yourself time to think through the decision you propose to make. And confirm that it is logical and fully justified.

10 *Consider the potential consequences* – McKinsey calls this 'consequence management'. Every decision has a consequence, and you should consider very carefully what that might be and how you will manage it. When making a decision it is a good idea to start from where you mean to end – define the end result and then work out the steps needed to achieve it.

Endnote

1 Drucker, P (1967) *The Effective Executive*, Heinemann, London

How to solve problems   36

Problems and opportunities

It is often said that 'there are no problems, only opportunities'. This is not universally true, of course, but it does emphasize the point that a problem should lead to positive thinking about what is to be done now, rather than to recriminations. If a mistake has been made, the reasons for it should be analysed, to ensure that it does not happen again. But it is then water under the bridge.

Faced with a continuous flow of problems you may occasionally feel utterly confused. We all feel like that sometimes.

Improving your skills

How can you improve your ability to solve problems? There are a few basic approaches you should use.

Improve your analytical ability

A complicated situation can often be resolved by separating the whole into its component parts. Such an analysis should relate to facts, although, as Peter Drucker[1] points out, when trying to understand the root causes of a problem you may have to start with an opinion. Even if you ask people to search for the facts first, they will probably look for those facts that fit the conclusion they have already reached.

Opinions are a perfectly good starting point as long as they are brought out into the open at once and then tested against reality.

Analyse each hypothesis and pick out the parts that need to be studied and tested.

Mary Parker Follett's[2] (1924) 'law of the situation' – the logic of facts and events – should rule in the end. And although you may start out with a hypothesis, when testing it use Rudyard Kipling's six honest serving men:

> I keep six honest serving men
>
> (They taught me all I knew)
>
> Their names are What and Why and When
>
> and How and Where and Who.

Use your imagination

A strictly logical answer to the problem may not be the best one. Use lateral thinking, analogies and brainstorming to get off your tramlines and dream up an entirely new approach.

Keep it simple

One of the first principles of logic is known as Occam's razor. It states that 'entities are not to be multiplied without necessity'. That is, always believe the simplest of several explanations.

Implementation

A problem has not been solved until the decision has been implemented. Think carefully not only about how a thing is to be done (by whom, with what resources and by when) but also about its impact on the people concerned and the extent to which they will cooperate. You will get less cooperation if you impose a solution. The best method is to arrange things so that everyone arrives jointly at a solution freely agreed to be the one best suited to the situation (the law of the situation again).

10 steps for effective problem-solving

1 *Define the situation* – establish what has gone wrong or is about to go wrong.

2 *Specify objectives* – define what is to be achieved now or in the future to deal with an actual or potential problem or change in circumstances.

3 *Develop hypotheses* – develop hypotheses about what has caused the problem.

4 *Get the facts* – find out what has actually happened and contrast this with an assessment of what ought to have happened. Try to understand the attitudes and motivation of those concerned. Remember that people will see what has happened in terms of their own position and feelings (their framework of reference). Obtain information about internal or external constraints that affect the situation.

5 *Analyse the facts* – determine what is relevant and what is irrelevant. Diagnose the likely cause or causes of the problem. Do not be tempted to focus on symptoms rather than root causes. Test any assumptions. Dig into what lies behind the problem.

6 *Identify possible courses of action* – spell out what each involves.

7 *Evaluate alternative courses of action* – assess the extent to which they are likely to achieve the objectives, the cost of implementation, any practical difficulties that might emerge and the possible reactions of stakeholders. Critical evaluation techniques can be used for this purpose.

8 *Weigh and decide* – determine which alternative is likely to result in the most practical and acceptable solution to the problem. This is often a balanced judgement.

9 *Plan implementation* – timetable project management resources required.

10 *Implementation* – monitor progress and evaluate success.

Endnotes

1 Drucker, P (1967) *The Effective Executive*, Heinemann, London

2 Follett, M P (1924) *Creative Experience*, Longmans Green, New York

How to innovate

37

Innovation is the lifeblood of an organization. There is nothing so stultifying to a company – or the people in it – as a belief that the old ways must be the best ways. An organization that tries to stand still will not survive.

Innovation requires a blend of creativity, clear thinking and the ability to get things done. It requires thinkers and doers to work closely together. Top management must create a climate in which managers have the scope to develop new ideas and the resources to implement them.

The success of innovative projects, therefore, can be seen to depend on two issues: the characteristics of the organization and those of the individual manager.

Organizational characteristics

The organizational characteristics that encourage innovation are:

- a free flow of information that allows executives to find ideas in unexpected places and pushes them to combine fragments of information;
- close and frequent contact between departments, and an emphasis on lateral as well as vertical relationships, providing resources, information and support;
- a tradition of working in teams and sharing credit;

- senior executives who believe in innovation and will make the necessary resources available;
- managers with the ability and desire to seize opportunities and to make time available for innovation.

Individual characteristics

To be an effective innovator you need:

- To have a clear initial view of the results you want to achieve – you should not worry too much to begin with about the ways of achieving them.
- To define clearly the aims and benefits of the project.
- To argue the case for the project persuasively, making a compelling business case (see Chapter 51).
- To elicit support not only from your boss but also from your colleagues and subordinates – you need to build a coalition in which everyone shares equally in the belief that the project is worthwhile.
- Courage – to take calculated risks and to weather the storm when the inevitable setbacks occur.
- To be good at getting people to act – mobilizing people to contribute fully to the project means using a participative management style.
- Power to mobilize support and resources and to achieve results.
- The ability to handle interference or opposition to the project – resistance can be open, but it often takes a passive or covert form: criticism of the plan's details, foot-dragging, late responses to requests, or arguments over the allocation of time and resources among projects. Covert resistance can be the most dangerous.
- The force of character to maintain momentum, especially after the initial enthusiasm for the project has waned and the team is involved in more tedious work.

How to conduct 38 a selection interview

The purpose of a selection interview

Selection interviews provide the information required to assess candidates against a person specification.

A selection interview should provide you with the answers to three fundamental questions:

1 Can the individual do the job? Is the person capable of doing the work to the standard required?

2 Will the individual do the job? Is the person well motivated?

3 How is the individual likely to fit into the team? Will I be able to work well with this person?

The nature of a selection interview

A selection interview should take the form of a conversation with a purpose. It is a conversation because candidates should be given the opportunity to talk freely about themselves and their careers. But the conversation has to be planned, directed and controlled to achieve your aims in the time available.

Your task as an interviewer is to draw candidates out to ensure that you get the information you want.

Candidates should be encouraged to do most of the talking – one of the besetting sins of poor interviewers is that they talk too much. But you have to plan the structure of the interview to achieve its purpose and decide in advance the questions you need to ask – questions that will give you what you need to make an accurate assessment:

Content – the information you want and the questions you ask to get it.

Contact – your ability to make and maintain good contact with candidates; to establish the sort of rapport that will encourage them to talk freely, thus revealing their strengths and their weaknesses.

Control – your ability to control the interview so that you get the information you want.

All this requires you to plan the interview thoroughly in terms of content, timing, structure and use of questions. But before doing all this you need to consider who is to conduct the interview and what arrangements need to be made for it.

Preparing for the interview

Initial preparations

Your first step in preparing for an interview should be to familiarize or refamiliarize yourself with the person specification, which defines the sort of individual you want in terms of qualifications, experience and personality. It is also advisable at this stage to prepare questions that you can put to all candidates so as to obtain the information you require. If you ask everyone some identical questions you will be able to compare the answers.

You should then read the candidates' CVs and application forms or letters. This will identify any special questions you should ask about their career or to fill in the gaps – 'What does this gap between jobs C and D signify?' (Although you would not put the question as baldly as that; it would be better to say something like this: 'I see there was a gap of six months between when you left your job in C and started in D. Would you mind telling me what you were doing during this time?')

Timing

You should decide at this stage how long you want to spend on each interview. As a rule of thumb, 45 to 60 minutes is usually required for serious, professional or technical appointments.

Middle-ranking jobs need about 30 to 45 minutes. The more routine jobs can be covered in 20 to 30 minutes. But the time allowed depends on the job and you do not want to insult a candidate by conducting a superficial interview.

The content of an interview

The content of an interview can be analysed by dividing it into three sections: the interview's beginning, middle and end.

Beginning

At the start of the interview you should put candidates at their ease. You want them to talk freely in response to your questions. They won't do this if you plunge in too abruptly. At least welcome them and thank them for coming to the interview, expressing genuine pleasure about the meeting. But don't waste too much time talking about their journey or the weather.

Some interviewers start by describing the company and the job. Wherever possible it is best to eliminate this part of the interview by sending candidates a brief job description and something about the organization. If you are not careful you will spend far too much time on this stage, especially if the candidate turns out to be clearly unsuitable. A brief reference to the job should suffice and this can be elaborated on at the end of the interview.

Middle

The middle part of the interview is where you find out what you need to know about candidates. It should take at least 80 per cent of the time, leaving, say, 5 per cent at the beginning and 15 per cent at the end. This is when you ask questions designed to provide information on:

- the extent to which the knowledge, skills, capabilities and personal qualities of candidates meet the person specification;
- the career history and ambitions of candidates and, sometimes, certain aspects of their behaviour at work such as sickness and absenteeism.

End

At the end of the interview you should give candidates the opportunity to ask questions about the job and the company. The quality of these questions can often give you clues about the degree to which applicants are interested and their ability to ask pertinent questions.

You may want to expand a little on the job. If candidates are promising, some interviewers at this stage extol the attractive features of the job. This is fine as long as these are not exaggerated. To give a 'realistic preview', the possible downsides should be mentioned, for example the need to travel, or unsocial working hours. If candidates are clearly unsuitable you can tactfully help them to deselect themselves by referring to aspects of the work that may not appeal to them, or for which they are not really qualified. It is best not to spell out these points too strongly. It is often sufficient simply to put the question: 'This is a key requirement of the job; how do you feel about it?' You can follow up this general question by more specific questions: 'Do you feel you have the right sort of experience?', 'Are you happy about (this aspect of the job)?'

At this stage you should ask final questions about the availability of candidates, as long as they are promising. You can ask when they would be able to start and about any holiday arrangements to which they are committed.

You should also ask their permission to obtain references from their present and previous employers. They might not want you to approach their present employer, and in that case you should tell them that if they are made an offer of employment it would be conditional on a satisfactory reference from their employer. It is useful to ensure that you have the names of people you can approach.

Finally, you inform candidates of what happens next. If some time could elapse before they hear from you, they should be told that you will be writing as soon as possible but that there will be some delay (don't make a promise you will be unable to keep).

It is not normally good practice to inform candidates of your decision at the end of the interview. You should take time to reflect on their suitability and you don't want to give them the impression that you are making a snap judgement.

Planning the interview

When planning interviews you should give some thought to how you are going to sequence your questions, especially in the middle part. There are two basic approaches, as described below.

Biographical approach

The biographical approach is probably the most popular because it is simple to use and appears to be logical. The interview can be sequenced chronologically, starting with the first job or even before that at school and, if appropriate, college or university.

The succeeding jobs, if any, are then dealt with in turn, ending with the present job, on which most time is spent if the candidate has been in it for a reasonable time. If you are not careful, however, using the chronological method for someone who has had a number of jobs can mean spending too much time on the earlier jobs, leaving insufficient time for the most important, recent experiences.

To overcome this problem, an alternative biographical approach is to start with the present job, which is discussed in some depth. The interviewer then works backwards, job by job, but only concentrating on particularly interesting or relevant experience in earlier jobs.

The problem with the biographical approach is that it is predictable. Experienced candidates are familiar with it and have their story ready, glossing over any weak points. It can also be unreliable. You can easily miss an important piece of information by concentrating on a succession of jobs rather than focusing on key aspects of the candidates' experience that illustrate their capabilities.

Criteria-based or targeted approach

This approach is often referred to as a structured interview. It is based on an analysis of the person specification. From this you can select the criteria on which you will judge the suitability of the candidate, and this will put you in a position to 'target' these key criteria during the interview. You can decide on the questions you need to ask in order to draw out from candidates information about their knowledge, skills, capabilities and personal qualities, which can be compared with the criteria to assess the extent to which candidates meet the specification.

This is probably the best way of focusing your interview to ensure that you get all the information you require about candidates for comparison with the person specification.

Interviewing techniques

Questioning

The most important interviewing technique you need to acquire and practise is questioning. Asking pertinent questions that elicit informative responses is a skill that people do not necessarily possess, but it is one they can develop. To improve your questioning techniques it is a good idea at the end of an interview to ask yourself: 'Did I ask the right questions?' 'Did I put them to the candidate well?' 'Did I get candidates to respond freely?'

There are a number of different types of questions, as described below. By choosing the right ones you can get candidates to open up or you can pin them down to giving you specific information or to extending or clarifying a reply. The other skills you should possess are the ability to establish rapport, and listening, maintaining continuity, keeping eye contact and note-taking.

The main types of questions are described below.

Open questions

Open questions are the best ones to use to get candidates to talk – to draw them out. These are questions that cannot be answered by a yes or no and that encourage a full response. Single-word answers are seldom illuminating. It is a good idea to begin the interview with one or two open questions, thus helping candidates to settle in.

Open-ended questions or phrases inviting a response can be phrased as follows:

- 'I'd like you to tell me about the sort of work you are doing in your present job.'
- 'What do you know about...?'
- 'Could you give me some examples of...?'
- 'In what ways do you think your experience fits you to do the job for which you have applied?'

Probing questions

Probing questions are used to get further details or to ensure that you are getting all the facts. You ask them when answers have been too generalized or when you suspect that there may be some more relevant information that candidates have not disclosed. A candidate may claim to have done something and it may be useful to find out more about exactly what contribution was made. Poor interviewers tend to let general and uninformative answers pass by without probing for further details, simply because they are sticking rigidly to a predetermined list of open questions. Skilled interviewers are able to flex their approach to ensure they get the facts while still keeping control to ensure that the interview is completed on time.

The following are some examples of probing questions:

- 'You've informed me that you have had experience in... Could you tell me more about what you did?'
- 'Could you describe in more detail the equipment you use?'
- 'What training have you had to operate your machine/equipment/ computer?'
- 'Why do you think that happened?'

Closed questions

Closed questions aim to clarify a point of fact. The expected reply will be an explicit single word or brief sentence. In a sense, a closed question acts as a probe but produces a succinct factual statement without going into detail. When you ask a closed question you intend to find out:

- What the candidate has or has not done – 'What did you do then?'
- Why something took place – 'Why did that happen?'
- When something took place – 'When did that happen?'
- How something happened – 'How did that situation arise?'
- Where something happened – 'Where were you at the time?'
- Who took part – 'Who else was involved?'

Capability questions

Capability questions aim to establish what candidates know, the skills they possess and use, and what they are capable of doing. They can be open, probing or closed but they will always be focused as precisely as possible on the contents of the person specification, referring to knowledge, skills and capabilities.

The sort of capability questions you can ask are:

- 'What do you know about...?'
- 'How did you gain this knowledge?'

- 'What are the key skills you are expected to use in your work?'
- 'How would your present employer rate the level of skill you have reached in...?'
- 'What do you use these skills to do?'
- 'How often do you use these skills?'
- 'What training have you received to develop these skills?'
- 'Could you please tell me exactly what sort and how much experience you have had in...?'
- 'Could you tell me more about what you have actually been doing in this aspect of your work?'
- 'Can you give me some examples of the sort of work you have done that would qualify you to do this job?'
- 'Could you tell me more about the machinery, equipment, processes or systems that you operate/for which you are responsible?' (The information could refer to such aspects as output or throughput, tolerances, use of computers or software, technical problems.)
- 'What are the most typical problems you have to deal with?'
- 'Would you tell me about any instances when you have had to deal with an unexpected problem or a crisis?'

Unhelpful questions

There are two types of questions that are unhelpful:

- *Multiple questions* such as 'What skills do you use most frequently in your job? Are they technical skills, leadership skills, teamworking skills or communicating skills?' will only confuse candidates. You will probably get a partial or misleading reply. Ask only one question at a time.

- *Leading questions* that indicate the reply you expect are also unhelpful. If you ask a question such as 'That's what you think, isn't it?', you will get the reply 'Yes, I do.' If you ask a question such as 'I take it that you don't really believe that...?', you will get the reply 'No, I don't.' Neither of these replies will get you anywhere.

Questions to be avoided

Avoid any questions that could be construed as being biased on the grounds of sex, race, disability or age.

10 useful questions

The following are 10 useful questions from which you can select any that are particularly relevant in an interview you are conducting:

1 'What are the most important aspects of your present job?'

2 'What do you think have been your most notable achievements in your career to date?'

3 'What sort of problems have you successfully solved recently in your job?'

4 'What have you learnt from your present job?'

5 'What has been your experience in...?'

6 'What do you know about...?'

7 'What is your approach to handling...?'

8 'What particularly interests you in this job and why?'

9 'Now you have heard more about the job, would you please tell me which aspects of your experience are most relevant?'

10 'Is there anything else about your career that hasn't come out yet in this interview but you think I ought to hear?'

Assessing the data

If you have carried out a good interview, you should have the data to assess the extent to which candidates meet each of the key points in the person specification. You can summarize your assessments by marking candidates against each of the points – 'exceeds specification', 'fully meets specification', 'just meets the minimum specification', 'does not meet the minimum specification'.

You can assess motivation broadly as 'highly motivated', 'reasonably well motivated', 'not very well motivated'.

You should also draw some conclusions from the candidates' career history and the other information you have gained about their behaviour at work. Credit should be given for a career that has progressed steadily, even if there have been several job changes. But a lot of job-hopping for no good reason and without making progress can lead you to suspect that a candidate is not particularly stable. No blame should be attached to a single setback – it can happen to anyone. Redundancy is not a stigma – it is happening all the time. But if the pattern is repeated, you can reasonably be suspicious.

Finally, there is the delicate question of whether you think you will be able to work with the candidate, and whether you think he or she will fit into the team. You have to be very careful about making judgements about how you will get on with someone. But if you are absolutely certain that the chemistry will not work, then you have to take account of that feeling, as long as you ensure that you have reasonable grounds for it on the basis of the behaviour of the candidate at the interview. But be aware of the common mistakes that interviewers can make. These include:

- jumping to conclusions on the basis of the first impression made by candidates – they may be personable, confident and outgoing and these characteristics may be important in some jobs, but the front people put up at an interview can disguise factors such as inadequate experience which could lead to failure in the job;

- jumping to conclusions on a single piece of favourable evidence – the 'halo effect';

- jumping to conclusions on a single piece of unfavourable evidence – the 'horns effect';

- not weighing up the balance between the favourable and unfavourable evidence logically and objectively;

- coming to firm conclusions on the basis of inadequate evidence;

- making snap or hurried judgements;

- making prejudiced judgements on the grounds of sex, race, disability, religion, appearance, accent, class, or any aspect of the candidate's life history, circumstances or career that do not fit your preconceptions of what you are looking for.

Coming to a conclusion

Compare your assessment of each of the candidates against one another. If any candidate fails in an area that is critical to success, he or she should be rejected. You can't take a chance. Your choice should be made between the candidates who reach an acceptable standard against each of the criteria. You can then come to an overall judgement, by reference to their assessments under each heading and their career history, as to which one is most likely to succeed.

In the end, your decision between qualified candidates may well be judgemental. There may be one outstanding candidate, but quite often there are two or three. In these circumstances you have to come to a balanced view on which one is more likely to fit the job *and* the organization and have potential for a long-term career, if this is possible. Don't, however, settle for second best in desperation. It is better to try again.

Remember to make and keep notes of the reasons for your choice and why candidates have been rejected. These, together with the applications, should be kept for at least six months just in case your decision is challenged as being discriminatory.

How to be interviewed for a job

Just as there are skills in selection interviewing, as described in Chapter 38, there are skills in being interviewed – making the right impression and responding to questions in a way that convinces the interviewer that you are the right person for the job. This chapter provides advice on the basic approaches you can adopt when being interviewed that, while none will guarantee that you will get the job, will all help to improve your chances. These approaches are concerned with:

- preparing for the interview;
- creating the right impression;
- responding to questions;
- ending on a high note.

Preparing for the interview

The first thing to remember when preparing for the interview is that you would not have been asked to attend unless you at least matched the basic specification. This should give you the confidence to plan how best to build on that foundation. You need to answer the following questions:

- *What have I got to offer that is likely to put me in a strong position to get this job?* Answer this by studying what you know about the job from the advertisement or, ideally, a more detailed specification produced by the prospective employers. This should give you some idea of what they are looking for.

- *How should I present my qualifications for the job?* Answer this by preparing a brief 40- or 50-word statement that sums up what you have to offer, what your ambitions are and why you want this job. This can be your point of reference throughout the interview, and you can use it as the basis for more detailed descriptions of your achievements and experience, accompanied by explanations of why these are relevant. Such a statement might read like this:

  > I am an experienced project manager with a proven track record of delivering projects on time, to specification and within budget. My achievements in a company operating in broadly the same field as yours fit me for the senior management position we are discussing.

- *What answers might I give to some typical questions?* For example:

  - Why do you want this job?
  - Tell me about yourself.
  - What have been your major achievements in your present job?
  - What are your strengths?
  - What are your weaknesses?
  - What do you think you would bring to this job?
  - What interests you most in your work?
  - Tell me about a time when you successfully dealt with a major problem at work.
  - What are your ambitions for the future?
  - What are your interests outside work?

Some of the material for answers to these questions should be found outlined in your statement. You may have to think how you would elaborate on it, but don't try to learn answers by heart. You have to appear spontaneous and, in any case, you cannot be sure that these questions will be asked in the same form (although it would be an unusual interview if none of them appeared in one shape or another).

Creating the right impression

First impressions in interviews count. Interviewers tend (often wrongly) to allow their initial reaction to you to colour the whole interview. It is said that many of them make up their minds in the first 30 seconds of the interview. So you must try to present yourself well from the very start. The things you can do include:

- dressing the part – neat, not gaudy;
- walking confidently into the room;
- giving a firm handshake and making eye contact;
- providing non-verbal clues such as smiling (but not a foolish grin), responding to the interviewer by nodding your head, leaning forward while listening and replying;
- sitting as far back on the chair as you can, not slumping;
- looking at the interviewer, maintaining a high level of eye contact.

From the start you have to give the impression of self-confidence. This is what interviewers are always looking for. And throughout the interview the way you respond to questions should convey your confidence in your own ability and your suitability for the job. The more articulate you are, without being glib, the better.

Responding to questions

A good interviewer will ask you open questions that will encourage you to talk and reveal your strengths and weaknesses. Some people talk themselves out of a job, so be careful not to over-elaborate. Make your replies as concise, clear and self-confident as possible.

Use positive language and provide positive information. You have to present your case convincingly. If you prefix your answers with a phrase such as 'I feel', 'I think' or 'Perhaps' you weaken your position. However, there is a danger of appearing too boastful or egotistical if you constantly blow your own trumpet and use 'I' to start every sentence.

Although it may be more powerful to say 'I did' rather than 'We did', it is possible to reduce the impression of egotism by using phrases such as 'My experience shows that I...', 'Colleagues tell me that...', 'My boss once remarked that...' or 'The team I was leading was able to...'

One of the trickiest questions you may be asked is about your weaknesses. You cannot claim that you have none (no one will believe you). Remember that negative information carries more weight with interviewers than positive information. Although interviewers usually ask about weaknesses (plural), you should only ever admit to one.

The approach you should adopt is to respond to questions, not answer them, by which is meant that you should control the information you release about yourself. To illustrate this approach, the answer to a question about weaknesses should be along the following lines:

- choose a trait about your character or personality that is obviously true;
- extend that trait until it becomes a fault;
- put it back in the distant past;
- show how you have overcome it;
- confirm that it is no longer a problem.

Ending on a high note

You will often be asked if you have any questions at the end of an interview. Do not bore the interviewer with trivial questions about the organization or the job. Instead ask positive questions that tacitly assume that the job is yours, such as 'What would be my priorities when (not if) I join you?' and 'What would you expect me to achieve in my first year?'

How to listen   40

There are many good writers and speakers but few good listeners. Most of us filter the spoken words addressed to us so that we absorb only some of them – frequently those we want to hear. Listening is an art that not many people cultivate. But it is a very necessary one, because a good listener will gather more information and achieve better rapport with the other person. And both these effects of good listening are essential to good communication.

People don't listen effectively because they are:

- unable to concentrate, for whatever reason;
- too preoccupied with themselves;
- over-concerned with what they are going to say next;
- uncertain about what they are listening to or why they are listening to it;
- unable to follow the points or arguments made by the speaker;
- simply not interested in what is being said.

Effective listeners:

- concentrate on the speaker, following not only words but also body language, which, through the use of eyes or gestures, often underlines meaning and gives life to the message;
- respond quickly to points made by the speaker, if only in the shape of encouraging grunts;
- ask questions frequently to elucidate meaning and to give the speaker an opportunity to rephrase or underline a point;
- comment on the points made by the speaker, without interrupting the flow, in order to test understanding and demonstrate that the speaker and listener are still on the same wavelength – these

comments may reflect back or summarize something the speaker has said, thus giving an opportunity for him or her to reconsider or elucidate the point made;

- make notes on the key points – even if the notes are not referred to later they will help to concentrate the mind;

- are continuously evaluating the messages being delivered to check that they are understood and relevant to the purpose of the meeting;

- are alert at all times to the nuances of what the speaker is saying;

- do not slump in their chair – they lean forward, show interest and maintain contact through their oral responses and by means of body language;

- are prepared to let the speaker go on with the minimum of interruption.

How to communicate

41

People recognize the need to communicate but find it difficult. Like Schopenhauer's hedgehogs, they want to get together; it's only their prickles that keep them apart.

Words may sound or look precise, but they are not. All sorts of barriers exist between the communicator and the receiver. Unless these barriers are overcome, the message will be distorted or will not get through.

Barriers to communication

Hearing what we want to hear

What we hear or understand when someone speaks to us is largely based on our own experience and background. Instead of hearing what people have told us, we hear what our minds tell us they have said. We have preconceptions about what people are going to say, and if what they say does not fit into our framework of reference we adjust it until it does. (Advice on how to listen is given in Chapter 40.)

Ignoring conflicting information

We tend to ignore or reject communication that conflicts with our own beliefs. If it is not rejected, some way is found of twisting and shaping its meaning to fit our preconceptions.

When a message is inconsistent with existing beliefs, the receiver rejects its validity, avoids further exposure to it, easily forgets it and, in his or her memory, distorts what has been heard.

Perceptions about the communicator

It is difficult to separate what we hear from our feelings about the person who says it. Non-existent motives may be ascribed to the communicator. If we like people we are more likely to accept what they say – whether it is right or wrong – than if we dislike them.

Influence of the group

The group with which we identify influences our attitudes and feelings. What a group hears depends on its interests. Workers are more likely to listen to their colleagues, who share their experiences, than to outsiders such as managers or union officials.

Words mean different things to different people

Essentially, language is a method of using symbols to represent facts and feelings. Strictly speaking, we can't convey meaning – all we can do is to convey words. Do not assume that because something has a certain meaning to you, it will convey the same meaning to someone else.

Non-verbal communication

When we try to understand the meaning of what people say, we listen to the words but we also use other clues that convey meaning. We attend not only to what people say but to how they say it. We form impressions from what is called body language – eyes, the shape of the mouth, the muscles of the face, even posture.

We may feel that these tell us more about what someone is really saying than the words he or she uses. But there is enormous scope for misinterpretation.

Emotions

Our emotions colour our ability to convey or to receive the true message. When we are insecure or worried, what we hear seems more threatening than when we are secure and at peace with the world. When we are angry or depressed, we tend to reject what might otherwise seem like reasonable requests or good ideas.

In a heated argument, many things that are said may not be understood or may be badly distorted.

Noise

Any interference to communication is 'noise'. It can be literal noise that prevents the message being heard, or figurative in the shape of distracting or confused information that distorts or obscures the meaning.

Size

The larger and more complex the organization, the greater the problem of communication. The more levels of management and supervision a message has to pass through, the greater the opportunity for distortion or misunderstanding.

Overcoming barriers to communication

Adjust to the world of the receiver

Try to predict the impact of what you are going to write or say on the receiver's feelings and attitudes. Tailor the message to fit the receiver's vocabulary, interests and values. Be aware of how the information might be misinterpreted because of prejudices, the influence of others and the tendency of people to reject what they do not want to hear.

Use feedback

Ensure that you get a message back from the receiver that tells you how much has been understood.

Use face-to-face communication

Whenever possible talk to people rather than e-mail or write to them. That is how you get feedback. You can adjust or change your message according to reactions. You can also deliver it in a more human and understanding way – this can help to overcome prejudices.

Verbal criticism can often be given in a more constructive manner than a written reproof, which always seems to be harsher.

Use reinforcement

You may have to present your message in a number of different ways to get it across. Re-emphasize the important points and follow up.

Use direct, simple language

This seems obvious. But many people clutter up what they say with jargon, long words and elaborate sentences.

Suit the actions to the word

Communications have to be credible to be effective. There is nothing worse than promising the earth and then failing to deliver. When you say you are going to do something, do it. Next time you are more likely to be believed.

Use different channels

Some communications have to be in writing to put the message across promptly and without any variations in the way they are delivered. But, wherever possible, supplement written communications with the spoken word. Conversely, an oral briefing should be reinforced in writing.

Reduce problems of size

If you can, reduce the number of levels of management.

Encourage a reasonable degree of informality in communications. Ensure that activities are grouped together to ease communication on matters of mutual concern.

How to make effective presentations   42

A manager's job usually includes giving formal or informal presentations at meetings, and addressing groups of people at conferences or training sessions. To be able to speak well in public is therefore a necessary management skill that you should acquire and develop.

The four keys to effective speaking are:

- overcoming nervousness;
- thorough preparation;
- good delivery;
- appropriate use of visual aids (especially PowerPoint).

Overcoming nervousness

Some nervousness is a good thing. It makes you prepare, makes you think and makes the adrenalin flow, thus raising performance. But excessive nervousness ruins your effectiveness and must be controlled.

The common reasons for excessive nervousness are fear of failure, fear of looking foolish, fear of breakdown, a sense of inferiority and dread of the isolation of the speaker. To overcome it there are three things to remember and six things to do.

Three things to remember about nervousness

1 Everyone is nervous. It is natural and, for the reasons mentioned earlier, a good thing.

2 Speaking standards are generally low. You can do better than the other person.

3 You have something to contribute. Otherwise why should you have been asked to speak?

Six things to do about nervousness

1 Practise. Take every opportunity you can get to speak in public. The more you do it, the more confident you will become. Solicit constructive criticism and act on it.

2 Know your subject. Get the facts, examples and illustrations that you need to put across.

3 Know your audience. Who is going to be there? What are they expecting to hear? What will they want to get out of listening to you?

4 Know your objective. Make sure that you know what you want to achieve. Visualize, if you can, each member of your audience going away having learned something new that he or she is going to put into practical use.

5 Prepare.

6 Rehearse.

Preparation

Allow yourself ample time for preparation in two ways. First, leave yourself plenty of low-pressure time; start thinking early – in your bath, on the way to work, while mowing your lawn, any place where you can freely develop new ideas on the subject. Second, you should leave yourself lots of time to actually prepare the talk. There are eight stages of preparation.

1 Agreeing to talk

Do not agree to talk unless you know you have something to contribute to this audience on this subject.

2 Getting informed

Collect facts and arguments for your talk by: brainstorming and writing down all the points as they occur; reading up on the subject; talking to colleagues and friends; and keeping cuttings and files on subjects you may have to speak on.

3 Deciding what to say

Start by defining your objective. Is it to persuade, inform, interest or inspire? Then decide the main message you want to put across. Adopt the 'rule of three'. Few people can absorb more than three new ideas at a time. Simplify your presentation to ensure that the three main points you want to convey come over loud and clear. Finally, select the facts and arguments that best support your message.

Never try to do too much. The most fatal mistake speakers can make is to tell everything they know. Select and simplify using the rule of three.

4 Structuring your presentation

Good structure is vital. It provides for continuity, makes your thoughts easy to follow, gives the talk perspective and balance, and, above all, enables you to ram your message home.

The classic method of structuring a talk is to: 'Tell them what you are going to say – say it – tell them what you have said.' This is the rule of three in action again, as applied to attention span. Your audience will probably only listen to one-third of what you say. If you say it three times in three different ways they will at least hear you once.

You were no doubt told at school that an essay should have a beginning, a middle and an end. Exactly the same principle applies to a talk.

Tackle the middle of your talk first and:

● write each main message on a separate postcard;

● list the points you want to make against each main message;

- illustrate the points with facts, evidence and examples, and introduce local colour;

- arrange the cards in different sequences to help you to decide on the best way to achieve impact and a logical flow of ideas.

Then turn to the opening of your talk. Your objectives should be to create attention, arouse interest and inspire confidence. Give your audience a trailer to what you are going to say. Underline the objective of your presentation – what they will get out of it.

Finally, think about how you are going to close your talk. First and last impressions are very important. End on a high note.

Think carefully about length, reinforcement and continuity. Never talk for more than 40 minutes at a time. Twenty to 30 minutes is better. Very few speakers can keep people's attention for long. An audience is usually very interested to begin with (unless you make a mess of your opening), but interest declines steadily until people realize that you are approaching the end. Then they perk up. Hence the importance of your conclusion.

To keep their attention throughout, give interim summaries that reinforce what you are saying and, above all, hammer home your key points at intervals throughout your talk.

Continuity is equally important. You should build your argument progressively until you come to a positive and overwhelming conclusion. Provide signposts, interim summaries and bridging sections that lead your audience naturally from one point to the next.

5 Prepare your notes

Your notes will be based on what you have already prepared. If you are giving a talk without the use of PowerPoint you can record your notes (the main messages and the supporting bullet points) on postcards so that they can easily be referred to in your presentation. It is often a good idea to write out your opening and closing remarks in full and then learn them by heart so that you can begin and end confidently. Clearly, they both have to be succinct.

If you are using PowerPoint (most people do), the text on the slides should correspond to the main points you want to make, with the proviso that you do not overload the slides (see penultimate section in this chapter). You can then print the PowerPoint slides full size and use them as your notes, with some brief and easily read annotations if you need them. The slides can also serve as handouts. Audiences are accustomed to these and no longer expect lots of prose, which they don't read anyhow.

At conferences, it is usual to issue the handouts in advance. This can be slightly disconcerting to the speaker, as members of the audience may bury their heads in the handouts and appear to be paying little attention to what is being said. Some speakers insist on the handouts being issued after the presentation, but this is not always allowed by the conference organizer. In these circumstances, it is up to you to make what you say as interesting as possible so the audience does pay attention.

6 Prepare visual aids

As your audience will only absorb one-third of what you say, if that, reinforce your message with visual aids. Appeal to more than one sense at a time. PowerPoint slides provide good backup, but don't overdo them and keep them simple. Too many visuals can be distracting, and too many words, or an over-elaborate presentation, will distract, bore and confuse your audience. (See penultimate section of this chapter on the uses and abuses of PowerPoint.)

7 Rehearse

Rehearsal is vital. It instils confidence, helps you to get your timing right, enables you to polish your opening and closing remarks and to coordinate your talk and visual aids.

Rehearse the talk to yourself several times and note how long each section takes. Get used to expanding your notes without waffling. Never write down your talk in full and read it during rehearsal. This will guarantee a stilted and lifeless presentation.

Practise giving your talk out loud – standing up, if that is the way you are going to present it. Some people like to tape record themselves but that can be off-putting. It is better to get someone to hear you and provide constructive criticism. It may be hard to take but it could do you a world of good.

Finally, try to rehearse in the actual room in which you are going to speak, using your visual aids and with someone listening at the back to make sure you are audible.

8 Check and prepare arrangements on site

Check the visibility of your visual aids. Make sure that you know how to use them. Test the projector. Brief your projector operator and get them to run through the slides to ensure there are no snags.

Be prepared for something to go wrong with your equipment. You may have to do without it at short notice. That is why you should not rely too much on visual aids.

Before you start your talk, check that your notes and visual aids are in the right order and to hand. There is nothing worse than a speaker who mixes up their speech and fumbles helplessly for the next slide.

Delivery

With thorough preparation you will not fail. You will not break down. But the way you deliver the talk will affect the impact you make. Good delivery depends on technique and manner.

Technique

Your *voice* should reach the people at the back. If you don't know that you can be heard, ask. It is distracting if someone shouts 'speak up'. Vary the pace, pitch and emphasis of your delivery. Pause before making a key point, to highlight it, and again afterwards to allow it to sink in. Try to be conversational. Avoid a stilted delivery. This is one reason why you should never read your talk. If you are your natural self the audience is more likely to be on your side.

Light relief is a good thing if it comes naturally. People are easily bored if they feel they are being lectured at, but you should never tell jokes unless you are good at telling jokes. Don't drag them in because you feel you must. Many effective and enjoyable speakers never use them.

Your *words* and *sentences* should be simple and short.

Your *eyes* are an important link with your audience. Look at them, measure their reaction and adjust to it. Don't fret if people look at their watches; it's when they start shaking them to see if they've stopped that you should start to worry!

Use *hands* for gesture and emphasis only. Avoid fidgeting. Don't put your hands in your pockets.

Stand naturally and upright. Do not stand casually. Be and look like someone in command. If you pace up and down like a caged tiger you will distract your audience. They will be waiting for you to trip over some equipment or fall off the edge of the platform.

Manner

Relax and show that you are relaxed. Convey an air of quiet confidence. Relaxation and confidence will come with thorough preparation and practice. At the beginning of your presentation look around at the audience and smile at them.

Don't preach or pontificate to your audience. They will resent it and turn against you.

Show sincerity and conviction. Obvious sincerity, belief in your message, positive conviction and enthusiasm in putting your message across count more than any technique.

Using PowerPoint

Most speakers rely on PowerPoint to back up their presentations. The slides are easy to prepare and because they enforce the use of bullet points, they encourage the development of succinct and easily followed expositions and arguments. They also enable handouts to be produced easily. But PowerPoint slides can be over-used, and present a number of dangers that can reduce rather than enhance the impact of a presentation. The following are 10 guidelines on their preparation and use:

1   Don't use too many slides. It's very tempting as they are so easy to prepare, but if they proliferate they can divert the attention of the audience from the key points you want to make (remember the rule of three). In a 40-minute presentation you should aim to keep the number of slides down to 15 or so – never more than 20. And the number should be reduced pro rata for shorter talks.

2   Don't clutter up the slides with too many words. The rule of six should be adopted – no more than six bullet points and no more than six words per bullet point. Keeping slides down to this number concentrates the mind wonderfully.

3   Make the font size as large as possible (another good reason for keeping the number of words to a minimum). Try to ensure that the heading is not less than 32 points and the text not less than 24 points. Ensure that the text can be seen against whatever background you select (yellow text on a deepish blue background stands out quite well).

4   Use diagrams wherever you can, on the basis that every picture can tell a story better than a host of words. Diagrams break up the presentation. There is nothing more boring than a succession of slides that are entirely bullet-pointed.

5   Use the PowerPoint facility for cascading bullet points (custom animation/appear) with discretion. It offers the advantage of making sure that each point can be dealt with in turn and is thus given greater significance. If the whole list of points is displayed at once the audience will be tempted to read it as a whole rather than listening to each point separately. But cascading every list of bullet points can bore and distract the audience. Save this approach for slides in which you have to elaborate on each point separately. Also, use the other PowerPoint facilities with discretion. The 'fly' facility provides a variation in the

way in which bullet points are presented to an audience, but does not add much if you use it every time. It is also helpful if you want to build up a diagram or flow chart to emphasize the sequence of points, but overdoing it can be messy and create confusion. It is tempting to use the 'dissolve' facility to provide elegant variation, but again, it can simply distract an audience who have come to hear what you have to say rather than to be present at a demonstration of PowerPoint tricks.

6   Do not try to be either too slick or too clever. Consultants often make this mistake when making presentations to clients. They attempt to overwhelm their audience with an over-sophisticated presentation and the people subjected to it are not impressed. They may prefer presenters who can get their points across without being propped up by PowerPoint – it shows that they can express themselves without resource to a visual aid. There is often a reaction against over-slick or clever-clever presentations.

7   PowerPoint slides provide useful notes, but don't just read them out point by point. Your audience may well ask themselves the question: 'What's the use of listening to this person who is simply telling me something that I can equally well read?'

8   It is sometimes a good idea to show a slide with a series of bullet points and give the audience the chance to read it. Then elaborate as necessary or, better still, get some participation by encouraging them to make comments or ask questions.

9   Never use the pre-packaged PowerPoint presentations. It always shows and it reveals the speaker as someone who cannot think of anything original to say. Never use other people's slides. You need to present your own ideas, not theirs.

10 Rehearse using the slides (or the handouts if you do not have a projector) to ensure that you can elaborate as necessary, and to indicate where you might get the audience to read them, with follow-up questions from yourself. You must be quite clear about the sequence of slides, and it is a good idea to prepare bridging remarks in advance to link slides together. A succession of unconnected slides will not impress.

Conclusions

- You can learn to become an effective speaker with practice. Seize every opportunity to develop your skills.

- Nervousness can be controlled by preparation and knowledge of technique.

- Good preparation is more than half the battle.

- Technique is there to help you to exploit your personality and style to the full, not to obliterate them.

How to write reports

The ability to express oneself clearly on paper and to write effective reports is one of a manager's most important skills. As often as not, it is through the medium of reports that you will convey your ideas and recommendations to your superiors and colleagues and inform them of the progress you are making.

What makes a good report?

The purpose of a report is to analyse and explain a situation, to propose and gain agreement to a plan. It should be logical, practical, persuasive and succinct.

To be an effective report writer you start by having something worthwhile to say. Clear thinking, creative thinking and problem-solving techniques will all help. Your analysis of opinions and facts and your evaluation of options should provide a base for positive conclusions and recommendations.

There are three fundamental rules for report writing:

1 give your report a logical structure;

2 use plain words to convey your meaning;

3 remember the importance of good, clear presentation of material.

Structure

A report should have a beginning, a middle and an end. If the report is lengthy or complex it will also need a summary of conclusions and recommendations. There may also be appendices containing detailed data and statistics.

Beginning

Your introduction should explain why the report has been written, its aims, its terms of reference, and why it should be read. It should then state the sources of information upon which the report was based. Finally, if the report is divided into various sections, the arrangement and labelling of these sections should be explained.

Middle

The middle of the report should contain the facts you have assembled and your analysis of those facts. The analysis should lead logically to a diagnosis of the causes of the problem. The conclusions and recommendations included in the final section should flow from the analysis and diagnosis. One of the most common weaknesses in reports is that the facts do not lead naturally to the conclusions; the other is that the conclusions are not supported by the facts.

Summarize the facts and your observations. If you have identified alternative courses of action, set out the pros and cons of each, but make it quite clear which one you favour. Don't leave your readers in mid-air.

A typical troubleshooting report would start by analysing the present situation; it would then diagnose any problems or weaknesses in that situation, explaining why these have occurred before making proposals on ways of dealing with the problem.

End

The final section of the report should set out your recommendations, stating how each of them will help to achieve the stated aims of the report or overcome any weaknesses revealed by the analytical studies.

The benefits and costs of implementing the recommendations should then be explained. The next stage is to propose a firm plan for implementing the proposals – the programme of work, complete with deadlines and names of people who would carry it out. Finally, tell the recipient(s) of the report what action, such as approval of plans or authorization of expenditure, you would like them to take.

Summary

In a long or complex report it is very helpful to provide an executive summary of conclusions and recommendations. It concentrates the reader's mind and can be used as an agenda in presenting and discussing the report. It is useful to cross-reference the items to the relevant paragraphs or sections of the report.

Plain words

> If language is not correct, then what is said is not what is meant; if what is said is not what is meant, then what ought to be done remains undone. CONFUCIUS

The heading of this section is taken from Sir Ernest Gowers' *The Complete Plain Words*.[1] This book is required reading for anyone interested in report writing. Gowers' recommendations on how best to convey meaning without ambiguity, and without giving unnecessary trouble to the reader, are:

- Use no more words than are necessary to express your meaning, for if you use more you are likely to obscure it and to tire your reader. In particular, do not use superfluous adjectives and adverbs, and do not use roundabout phrases where single words would serve.

- Use familiar words rather than the far-fetched if they express your meaning equally well, for the familiar are more likely to be understood.

- Use words with a precise meaning rather than those that are vague, for they will obviously serve better to make your meaning clear; and in particular, prefer concrete words to abstract for they are more likely to have a precise meaning.

You will not go far wrong if you follow these precepts.

Presentation

The way in which you present your report affects its impact and value. The reader should be able to follow your argument easily and not get bogged down in too much detail.

Paragraphs should be short and each one should be restricted to a single topic. If you want to list or highlight a series of points, tabulate them or use bullet points. For example:

Pay reviews

Control should be maintained over increments by issuing guidelines to managers on:

- the maximum percentage increase to their payroll allowable for increments to individual salaries;

- the maximum percentage increase that should be paid to a member of staff.

Paragraphs may be numbered for ease of reference. Some people prefer the system that numbers main sections 1, 2, etc, subsections 1.1, 1.2, etc, and sub-sub-sections 1.1.1, 1.1.2, etc. However, this can be clumsy and distracting. A simpler system, which eases cross-referencing, is to number each paragraph, not the headings, 1, 2, 3, etc; sub-paragraphs or tabulations are identified as 1(a), 1(b), 1(c), etc and sub-sub-paragraphs if required as 1(a)(i), 1(a)(ii), 1(a) (iii), etc (or use bullet points).

Use headings to guide people on what they are about to read and to help them to find their way about the report. Main headings should be in capitals or bold and subheadings in lower case or italics.

A long report could have an index listing the main and subheadings and their paragraph numbers (as shown in Table 43.1).

Table 43.1   Report index

	Paragraphs
PAY ADMINISTRATION	83–92
Pay structure	84–88
Job evaluation	89–90
Pay reviews	91–92

Your report will make most impact if it is brief and to the point. Read and re-read your draft to cut out any superfluous material or flabby writing. Use bullet points to simplify the presentation and to put your messages across clearly and succinctly.

Do not clutter up the main pages of the report with masses of indigestible figures or other data. Summarize key statistics in compact, easy-to-follow tables with clear headings. Relegate supporting material to an appendix.

Endnote

1 Gowers, Sir E (1987) *The Complete Plain Words*, Penguin, London

How to network 44

Increasingly in today's more fluid and flexible organizations, people get things done by networking. Networks are loosely organized connections between people with shared interests. Networking takes place within them when people exchange information, enlist support and create alliances – getting agreement with other people on a course of action and joining forces to make it happen. It occurs outside the usual formal communication channels. It is an essential way of getting things done in organizations – it ensures that the informal organization works.

Networks inside organizations are often fluid and informal. They exist to meet a need but they can be dispersed if that need no longer exists, only to be reformed when it reappears. Networks may just consist of people with similar aims or interests who communicate with one another or get together as required. Networks are sometimes set up formally in organizations, for example the 'communities of interest' which are created to exchange and share knowledge and experience as part of a 'knowledge management' programme.

Networks can also exist outside the organization. Again, they may consist of like-minded individuals exchanging information and meeting informally, or they may be set up formally with regular meetings and newsletters.

To network effectively here are 10 steps you can take:

1   Identify people who may be able to help.

2   Seize any opportunity that presents itself to get to know people who may be useful.

3   Have a clear idea of why you want to network – to share knowledge, to persuade people to accept your proposal or point of view, to form an alliance.

4   Know what you can contribute – networking is not simply about enlisting support, it is just as much, if not more concerned with developing knowledge and understanding and joining forces with like-minded people so that concerted effort can be deployed to get things done.

5   Show interest – if you engage with people and listen to them they are more likely to want to network with you.

6   Ask people if you can help them as well as asking people to help you.

7   Put people in touch with one another.

8   Operate informally but be prepared to call formal meetings when necessary to reach agreement and plan action.

9   Make an effort to keep in touch with people.

10 Follow up – check with members of the network on progress in achieving something, refer back to conversations you have had, discuss with others how the network might be developed or extended to increase its effectiveness.

How to be strategic   45

It is often said that managers must be strategic if they want to get on. But what is the process of 'being strategic'? To answer this question it is necessary to understand what is meant by strategy and strategic management and, in the light of this understanding, to describe what managers do when they are being strategic.

What is strategy?

Strategy can be defined as the continuous process of defining a sense of purpose and direction. It aims to match the organization's capabilities and resources to the opportunities available in the external environment in the most advantageous way and to ensure that different aspects of the strategy cohere and are mutually supportive.

Strategy has often been defined as a logical, step-by-step affair, the outcome of which is a formal written statement that provides a definitive guide to the organization's long-term intentions. Many people still believe that this is the case, but it is a misrepresentation of reality. In practice the formulation of strategy is never the rational and linear process described by some writers or attempted by some managers. Strategies often tend to be fragmented, evolutionary and largely intuitive. They emerge in response to evolving situations in the shape of actions and reactions. This does not mean that a strategic approach to management as described below is inappropriate or unachievable. It may not be such a formal process as some people think but it is still desirable to assess continuously where you want to go and how you intend to get there and to consider how this can best fit in with the achievement of the organization's goals.

Strategic management

The purpose of strategic management as defined by Rosabeth Moss Kanter[1] is to 'elicit the present actions for the future' and become 'action vehicles – integrating and institutionalizing mechanisms for change'. The main concern of strategists is to identify the broader issues they are facing and decide on the general directions they must take to deal with these issues and achieve future business objectives. They do not take a narrow or restricted view.

Strategic management deals with both ends and means. As an end, it describes a vision of what something will look like in a few years' time. As a means, it shows how it is expected that the vision will be realized. Strategic management is visionary management, concerned with creating and conceptualizing ideas of where the organization should be going. But it is also empirical management that decides how in practice it is going to get there. This means getting things right now.

Businesses and managers must perform well in the present to succeed in the future. Strategic management is about the future but it is also about integrating activities now so that they are mutually supportive in the pursuit of immediate and longer-term goals.

Strategic managers

Managers who act strategically will think about what the organization wants to be and become and what they can do to ensure this happens. They will have a broad view of where they are going and are capable of seeing 'the big picture', looking beyond the confines of their immediate problems to what lies ahead and how what they do supports the efforts of other people. But they will also be aware that they are responsible, first, for planning how to allocate resources (people and money) in ways that contribute to the implementation of strategy, and second, for managing these resources so that they significantly add value to the results achieved by the firm.

10 things to do if you want to manage strategically

1 Understand the business and its competitive environment.

2 Be aware of the goals of the business and its plans to attain them.

3 Align what you are doing with the organization's business strategy.

4 Know where you are going and how you are going to get there.

5 Remember that formal strategic plans do not guarantee success; it is the implementation of the plans that delivers results.

6 Know how to plan the use of resources to make the best use of business opportunities.

7 Understand how you can contribute to the achievement of the objectives of the key functions in the business and support the strategic activities of your colleagues.

8 Be able to foresee longer-term developments, envisage options and their probable consequences, and select sound courses of action.

9 Rise above the day-to-day detail.

10 Challenge the status quo.

Endnote

1 Kanter, R M (1989) *When Giants Learn to Dance*, Simon & Schuster, London

How to think clearly

Clear thinking is logical thinking. It is a process of reasoning by which one judgement is derived from another and correct conclusions are drawn from the evidence. Clear thinking is analytical: sifting information, selecting what is relevant, establishing and proving relationships.

If you say people are logical, you mean that they draw reasonable inferences – their conclusions can be proved by reference to the facts used to support them. They avoid ill-founded and tendentious arguments, generalizations and irrelevancies. Their chain of reasoning is clear, unemotional and based on relevant facts.

Clear thinking – a logical approach to problem-solving, decision-making and case presentation – is an essential attribute of an effective manager. This does not mean that it is the only way to think. Edward de Bono has made out an incontrovertible case for lateral (ie creative) thinking as a necessary process for innovative managers to use alongside the more traditional vertical or logical thinking patterns. But a logical approach is still an essential requirement.

A further attribute of a good manager is the ability to argue persuasively and to detect the flaws in other people's arguments. To think clearly and to argue well, you need to understand: first, how to develop a proposition or a case from basic principles; second, how to test your proposition; third, how to avoid using fallacious arguments and how to expose the fallacies used by others; and finally, how to bring these techniques together into the process of critical thinking, a fundamental skill which it is essential that better managers possess.

Developing a proposition

The first rule is to 'get the facts'. It is the starting point for clear thinking. The facts must be relevant to the issue under consideration. If comparisons are being made, like must be compared with like. Trends must be related to an appropriate base date, and if trends are being compared, the same base should be used. Treat opinions with caution until they are supported by evidence. Avoid a superficial analysis of surface data. Dig deep. Take nothing for granted. Sift the evidence and discard what is irrelevant.

Your inferences should be derived directly from the facts. Where possible, the connection between the facts and the conclusion should be shown to be justified on the basis of verifiable and relevant experience or information on similar relationships occurring elsewhere.

If, as is likely, more than one inference can be deduced from the facts, you should test each inference to establish which one most clearly derives from the evidence as supported by experience. But it is no good saying 'it stands to reason' or 'it's common sense'. You have to practise evidence-based management, ie produce the evidence that proves that the inference is reasonable, and you have to pin down the vague concept of common sense to the data and experience upon which it is based. It was Descartes who wrote: 'Common sense is the best distributed commodity in the world, for every man is convinced that he is well supplied with it.'

Testing propositions

Susan Stebbing,[1] in *Thinking to Some Purpose*, wrote: 'We are content to accept without testing any belief that fits in with our prejudices and whose truth is necessary for the satisfaction of our desires.' Clear thinking must try to avoid this trap.

When we form a proposition or belief we generalize from what is observed – our own analysis or experience – and thence infer to what is not observed. We also refer to testimony – other people's observations and experience.

If your proposition or belief is derived from a generalization based upon particular instances, you should test it by answering the following questions:

- Was the scope of the investigation sufficiently comprehensive?
- Are the instances representative or are they selected to support a point of view?
- Are there contradictory instances that have not been looked for?
- Does the proposition or belief in question conflict with other beliefs for which we have equally good grounds?
- If there are any conflicting beliefs or contradictory items of evidence, have they been put to the test against the original proposition?
- Could the evidence or testimony lead to other, equally valid conclusions?
- Are there any other factors that have not been taken into account that may have influenced the evidence and, therefore, the conclusion?

If your belief is based on testimony, you should test the reliability of the testimony, its relevance to the point, and whether or not your belief follows logically from the evidence: that is, it can reasonably be inferred from the facts.

Fallacious and misleading arguments

A fallacy is an unsound form of argument leading to a mistake in reasoning or a misleading impression. The main fallacies to avoid or to spot in other people's arguments are:

- sweeping statements;
- potted thinking;
- special pleading;
- oversimplification;
- reaching false conclusions;

- begging the question;
- false analogy;
- using words ambiguously;
- chop logic.

These are discussed briefly below.

Sweeping statements

In our desire for certainty and to carry the point, we often indulge in sweeping statements. We sometimes then repeat them more and more loudly and angrily in order to convince our opponent. If we do it often enough and forcibly enough we can even deceive ourselves. It has been said that: 'It's never fair, it's never wise, it's never safe to generalize.' But that is a generalization in itself. Scientific method is based on generalizations. They can be valid if they are inferred properly from adequate, relevant and reliable evidence.

Generalizations are invalid when they have been produced by over-simplifying the facts or by selecting instances favourable to a contention while ignoring those that conflict with it. The classic form of a fallacious generalization is the contention that if some A is B then all A must be B. What frequently happens is that people say A is B when all they know is that some A is B or, at most, A tends to be B. The argument is misleading unless the word 'some' or 'tends' is admitted.

Many of the fallacies considered below are special cases of unsafe generalization, the most common symptom of unsound reasoning.

Potted thinking

Potted thinking happens when we argue using slogans and catch-phrases, when we extend an assertion in an unwarrantable fashion.

It is natural to form confident beliefs about complicated matters when we are proposing or taking action. And it is equally natural to compress these beliefs into a single phrase or thought. But it is dangerous to accept compressed statements that save us the trouble of thinking. They are only acceptable if fresh thinking has preceded them.

Special pleading

If people say to you, 'everyone knows that', 'it's obvious that' or 'it's indisputably true that', you can be certain that they have taken for granted what they are about to assert.

We indulge in special pleading when we stress our own case and fail to see that there may be other points of view, other ways of looking at the question. Special pleading happens when we cannot detach ourselves from our own circumstances. We often blunder because we forget that what is true of one of us is also true of the other in the same situation.

A safeguard against this mistake is to change 'you' into 'I'. Thus, I feel that you can't see what is straight in front of your nose; you feel that I can't see what is on the other side of my blinkers. A rule that appears to be sound when I apply it to you may seem to be unsatisfactory when you ask me to apply it to myself.

Of course, thinking for too long about other points of view is a recipe for indecision. There are not necessarily two sides to every question and even if there are, you eventually – and often quickly – have to come down firmly on one side. But before you do this, check in case the other points of view or the alternative approaches are valid, and take them into account.

Oversimplification

Oversimplification is a special form of potted thinking or special pleading. It often arises in the form of what Susan Stebbing terms 'the fallacy of either black or white', the mistake of demanding that a sharp line should be drawn, when in fact no sharp line can be drawn. For example, we cannot ask for a clear distinction to be drawn between the sane and the insane, or between the intelligent and the unintelligent. Our readiness to make this mistake may be taken advantage of by a dishonest opponent, who insists that we define precisely things that do not permit such definition.

Reaching false conclusions

One of the most prevalent fallacies is that of forming the view that because some are or may be, all are. An assertion about several cases is twisted into an assertion about all cases. The conclusion does not follow the premise.

The most common form of this fallacy is what logicians call the 'undistributed middle', which refers to the traditional syllogism consisting of a premise, a middle term and a conclusion.

A valid syllogism takes the following form:

Premise: All cows are quadrupeds.

Middle term: All quadrupeds are vertebrates.

Conclusion: Therefore, all cows are vertebrates.

This may be represented as:

Premise: All A is B.

Middle term: All B is C.

Conclusion: Therefore, all A is C.

This is logical. The middle term is fully distributed. Everything that applies to A also applies to B, everything that applies to B also applies to C, therefore everything that applies to A must apply to C.

An invalid syllogism would take the following form:

All cows are quadrupeds.

All mules are quadrupeds.

Therefore, all cows are mules.

This may be represented as:

All A is B.

All C is B.

Therefore, all A is C.

This is false because, although everything that applies to A and C also applies to B, there is nothing in their relationship to B that connects A and C together.

The difference between the true and false syllogism may be illustrated in Figure 46.1. In the false syllogism, A and C could be quite distinct although still contained within B. To link them together goes beyond the original evidence. The fact that two things, A and B, are related to another thing, C, does not necessarily mean that they are related together. In forming arguments, we too often jump to the conclusion that some means all.

Allowing the conclusion to go beyond the evidence can also take the form of assuming that because we are aware of the effect (the consequent), we also know the cause (the antecedent). But this assumption may be incorrect. An effect can have many different causes. This fallacy of the consequent, as it is termed, can be illustrated by the following example:

> If she won the lottery she would go to the West Indies.
>
> She has gone to the West Indies.
>
> Therefore she has won the lottery.
>
> ie If P then Q.
>
> Q.
>
> Therefore P.

Figure 46.1   The difference between true and false syllogisms

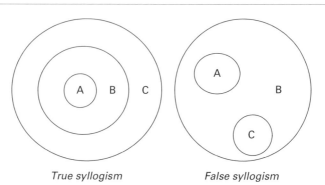

True syllogism   False syllogism

But there are a number of other reasons why she could have gone to the West Indies besides winning the lottery. A clear inference can only be drawn if the cause is directly related to the effect, thus:

> If she wins the lottery she will go to the West Indies.
>
> She has won the lottery.
>
> Therefore she will go to the West Indies.
>
> ie if P then Q.
>
> P.
>
> Therefore Q.

A further danger in drawing conclusions from evidence is to forget that circumstances may alter cases. What has happened in the past will not necessarily happen again unless the circumstances are the same. You may be able to infer something from history but you cannot rely on that inference. Times change.

Begging the question

We beg the question when we take for granted what has yet to be proved. This can take the form of assuming the point in dispute without adequate reason; what the logicians call *petitio principii*.

If you spot anyone taking for granted a premise that is not contained in the conclusion you must challenge the assumption and ask for information about the premises upon which the conclusion is based. You can then assess whether or not the conclusion follows logically from those premises.

Challenging assumptions is a necessary part of thinking clearly. You should challenge your own assumptions as well as those made by others.

False analogy

Analogy forms the basis of much of our thinking. We notice that two cases resemble each other in certain respects and then infer an extension of the resemblance. Analogies also aid understanding of an unfamiliar topic.

Analogies can be used falsely as vivid arguments without any real evidence. Just because A is B, where both are familiar matters of fact, does not mean that X is Y, where X and Y are unfamiliar or abstract. When we argue by analogy we claim that if:

X has properties of P1, P2, P3 and F,

and Y has properties of P1, P2 and P3,

therefore Y also has the property of F.

This could be true unless Y has a property incompatible with F, in which case the argument is unsound.

Analogies may be used to suggest a conclusion but they cannot establish it. They can be carried too far. Sometimes their relevance is more apparent than real.

Use argument by analogy to help support a case but do not rely upon it. Don't allow anyone else to get away with far-fetched analogies. They should be tested and their relevance should be proved.

Using words ambiguously

The Lewis Carroll approach – 'When I use a word it means just what I choose it to mean, neither more nor less' – is a favourite trick of those who aim to deceive. People use words that beg the question; that is, they define a word in a special way that supports their argument. They shift the meaning of words in different contexts. They may choose words that have the same meaning as each other but that show approval or disapproval.

There is a well-known saying that the word 'firm' can be declined as follows: 'I am firm, You are obstinate, He is pigheaded.'

Chop logic

'Contrariwise', continued Tweedledee, 'if it was so, it might be, and if it were so, it would be; but as it isn't, it ain't. That's logic.' LEWIS CARROLL

Chop logic is not quite as bad as that, but it can be equally misleading. It includes such debating tricks as:

- selecting instances favourable to a contention while ignoring those that conflict with it;

- twisting an argument advanced by opponents to mean something quite different from what was intended – putting words in someone's mouth;

- diverting opponents by throwing on them the burden of proving something they have not maintained;

- deliberately ignoring the point in dispute;

- introducing irrelevant matter into the argument;

- reiterating what has been denied and ignoring what has been asserted.

Critical thinking

Critical thinking is the process of analysing and evaluating the quality of ideas, theories and concepts to establish the degree to which they are valid and supported by the evidence and the extent to which they are biased. It involves reflecting on and interpreting data, drawing warranted conclusions and recognizing ill-defined assumptions. It is what managers do when they think clearly and purposefully.

'Critical' in this context does not mean disapproval or being negative. There are many positive uses of critical thinking, for example testing a hypothesis, proving a proposition or evaluating a concept, theory or argument. Critical thinking can occur whenever people weigh up evidence and make a judgement, solve a problem or reach a decision. The aim is to come to well-reasoned conclusions and solutions and to test them against relevant criteria and standards. Critical thinking calls for the ability to:

- recognize problems and establish ways of dealing with them;

- gather and marshal pertinent (relevant) information;

- identify unstated assumptions and values;

- interpret data, to appraise evidence and to evaluate arguments;

- recognize the existence (or non-existence) of logical relationships between propositions;
- draw warranted conclusions and make valid generalizations;
- test assertions, conclusions and generalizations;
- reconstruct ideas or beliefs by examining and analysing relevant evidence.

Endnote

1 Stebbing, S (1959) *Thinking to Some Purpose*, Penguin Books, Harmondsworth

How to troubleshoot 47

No matter what you do, things will sometimes go wrong. As a manager, you will often be called upon to put them right, or to employ other people to do it for you.

Troubleshooting requires: diagnostic ability, to size up the difficulties; know-how, to select the required solution and decide how to implement it; and managerial skill, to put the solution into effect. It can be divided into three main parts:

1 planning the campaign;

2 diagnosis;

3 cure.

Planning the campaign

Even if you decide to do it yourself without using management consultants, you can still take a leaf out of the consultant's book. A good management consultant will go through the following stages:

1 Analysis and diagnosis of the present situation: what has happened and why.

2 Development of alternative solutions to the problem.

3 Decision as to the preferred solution, stating the costs and benefits of implementing it.

4 Defining a method of proceeding: how and over what timescale the solution should be implemented, who does it and with what resources. If a staged implementation is preferred, the stages will be defined and a programme worked out.

The most important task at the planning stage is to define the problem, and clarify objectives and terms of reference. A problem defined is a problem half solved. And it is the difficult half. The rest should follow quite naturally if an analytical approach is adopted.

Once you know what the problem is you can define what you want done and prepare terms of reference for those who are conducting the investigation, including yourself. These should set out the problem, how and by whom it is to be tackled, what is to be achieved and by when. All those concerned in the exercise should know what these terms of reference are.

The next step is to programme the troubleshooting assignment. Four points need to be decided: the information you need, where you get it from, how you obtain it and who receives it. Draw up lists of facts required and the people who can supply them. Remember you will have to deal with opinion as well as fact; all data are subject to interpretation. List those who are likely to understand what has happened and why; those who might have good ideas about what to do next.

Then draw up your programme. Give notice that you require information. Warn people in plenty of time that you want to discuss particular points with them and that you expect them to have thought about the subject *and* have supporting evidence to hand.

Diagnosis

Diagnosis means finding out what is happening – the symptoms – and then digging to establish why it is happening – the cause. There may be a mass of evidence. The skilled diagnostician dissects the facts, sorts out what is relevant to the problem and refines it all down until he or she reveals the crucial pieces of information that show the cause of the problem and point to its solution.

Analytical ability – being able to sort the wheat from the chaff – is a key element in diagnosis. It is a matter of getting the facts and then submitting each one to a critical examination, in order to determine which is significant.

During the process of diagnosis, you must remain open-minded. You should not allow yourself to have preconceptions or to be over-influenced by anyone's opinion. Listen and observe, but suspend judgement until you can arrange all the facts against all the opinions.

At the same time, do whatever you can to enlist the interest and support of those involved. If you can minimize their natural fears and suspicions, those close to the problem will reveal ideas and facts that might otherwise be concealed from you.

Troubleshooting checklist

Base your diagnosis on an analysis of the factors likely to have contributed to the problem: people, systems, structure and circumstances.

People

- Have mistakes been made? If so, why? Is it because staff are inadequate in themselves or is it because they have been badly managed or trained?

- If management is at fault, is the problem one of system, structure or the managers themselves?

- If the people doing the job are inadequate, why were they selected in the first place?

Systems

- To what extent are poor systems or procedures to blame for the problem?

- Is the fault in the systems themselves? Are they badly designed or inappropriate?

- Or is it the fault of the people who operate or manage the systems?

Structure

- How far has the organization or management structure contributed to the problem?

- Do people know what is expected of them?

- Are activities grouped together logically, so that adequate control can be exercised over them?

- Are managers and supervisors clear about their responsibilities for maintaining control and do they exercise these responsibilities effectively?

Circumstances

- To what extent, if any, is the problem a result of circumstances beyond the control of those concerned? For example, have external economic pressures or changing government policies had a detrimental effect?

- If there have been external pressures, has there been a failure to anticipate or to react quickly enough to them?

- Have adequate resources (people, money and materials) been made available, and if not, why not?

Cure

The diagnosis should point the way to the cure. But this may still mean that you have to evaluate different ways of dealing with the problem. There is seldom 'one best way', only a choice between alternatives. You have to narrow them down until you reach the one that, *on balance*, is better than the others.

Your diagnosis should have established the extent to which the problem is one of people, systems, structure or circumstances. Fallible human beings may well be at the bottom of it. If so, remember not to indulge in indiscriminate criticism. Your job is to be constructive; to build people up, not to destroy them.

Avoid being too theoretical. Take account of circumstances – including the ability of the people available now to deal with the problem, or, if you have doubts, the availability of people from elsewhere who can be deployed effectively. Your recommendation should be practical in the sense that it can be made to work with resources that are readily available and within acceptable timescales.

You must make clear not only what needs to be done but how it is to be done. Assess costs as well as benefits and demonstrate that the benefits outweigh the costs. Resources have to be allocated, a timescale set and, above all, specific responsibility given to people to get the work done. Your recommendations have to be realistic in the sense that they can be phased in without undue disruption and without spending more time and money than is justified by the results.

Take care when you apportion blame to individuals. Some may clearly be inadequate and have to be replaced. Others may be the victims of poor management, poor training or circumstances beyond their control. Their help may be essential in overcoming the trouble. It is unwise to destroy their confidence or their willingness to help.

Using management consultants to troubleshoot

A management consultant has been described, or dismissed, as someone with a briefcase 50 miles from home. Robert Townsend[1] describes consultants as people 'who borrow your watch to tell you what time it is and then walk off with it'.

Calling in consultants in desperation can indeed be an expensive and time-wasting exercise. But they have their uses. They bring experience and expertise in diagnosis. They can act as an extra pair of hands when suitable people are not available from within the organization. And, as a third party, they can sometimes see the wood through the trees and solve problems or unlock ideas within the company that, sadly, are often inhibited by structural or managerial constraints.

There are, however, a number of rules, as set out in Table 47.1, which you should be aware of when contemplating bringing in consultants.

Table 47.1   Rules when contemplating bringing in consultants

Do	Don't
Get tenders from two or three firms and compare, not only their fees, but their understanding of your problem and the practical suggestions they have on how to tackle it.	Be bamboozled by a smooth principal who is employed mainly as a salesperson.
Check on the experience of the firm and, most important, of the consultant who is going to carry out the assignment.	Go for a big firm simply because it has a good reputation. It may not have the particular expertise you want.
Brief the firm very carefully on the terms of reference.	Accept any old consultant who comes along. Many redundant executives have set up as consultants without having a clue about how to do it. There is a lot of skill in being an effective consultant. Check that the firm is a member of the Management Consultants Association or that the principal is a member of the Institute of Management Consultancy (for UK-based firms). These provide a guarantee of professional status.
Get a clear statement of the proposed programme, total estimated costs (fees plus expenses) and who is actually going to carry out the assignment.	
Meet and assess the consultant who is going to carry out the work. Insist on regular progress meetings.	
Ensure that the outcome of the assignment is a practical proposal that you can implement yourself, or with the minimum of further help.	Allow the consultant to change the programme without prior consultation.
	Leave the consultant to his or her own devices for too long. Keep in touch. Appoint a member of your staff to liaise or even to work with the consultant.

Endnote

1   Townsend, R (1970) *Up the Organization*, Michael Joseph, London

How to recover from setbacks 48

Even good managers have setbacks during their career, but the best managers recover from them quickly and go on to do even better. Here are some comments on coping with a reverse in your fortunes:

- 'Ever tried. Ever failed. No matter. Try again. Fail again. Fail better.' (*Samuel Beckett*)
- 'Regret nothing that's happened.' (*Guy Browning*)
- 'The greater the difficulty, the more glory in surmounting it.' (*Epicurus*)

Capturing these and other thoughts, there are 10 things you can do to recover from a setback:

1 Learn from what has happened.

2 If you have made a mistake, analyse how and why you did and how you can avoid making it again.

3 Accentuate the positive and build on what you know and can do and have already achieved.

4 Assess your strengths and work out how you can use them more effectively in the future.

5 Assess your weaknesses (but don't dwell on them) and what you need to do to overcome them.

6 Although it is good to assess your strengths and weaknesses, avoid too much introspection – get into action.

7   Seek the views of those you respect on what action you should take.

8   Be clear about where you want to go and how you are going to get there.

9   Enlist support from others in achieving your plans.

10   Realize it's not the end of the world.

How things go   49
wrong and how
to put them right

Things can go wrong through events beyond your control or through incompetence. It is difficult and very rare for anyone to admit that they are incompetent, but this is why things most frequently go adrift. It is therefore useful to know something about the causes of incompetence so that you can put them right.

You should also know about troubleshooting as covered in Chapter 47, so that you can tackle problems, whether or not they are of your own making. Theodore Roosevelt once said: 'Do what you can, with what you have, where you are.' The trouble is, people don't always take this advice. Things go wrong because people do less than they are capable of, misuse their resources or choose an inappropriate time or place in which to do it. Situations are misjudged and the wrong action is taken.

Studies of incompetence

There have been two interesting analyses of incompetence that, if studied, will give you some clues about how to avoid or at least minimize mistakes. The first of these is *The Peter Principle* by Dr Lawrence J Peter;[1] the second is *On the Psychology of Military Incompetence* by Norman F Dixon.[2]

The Peter Principle

In *The Peter Principle*, Dr Lawrence Peter suggested that in a hierarchy, individuals tend to rise to the level of their own incompetence. This somewhat pessimistic view was based on his experience that the system encourages this to happen because people are told that if they are doing their job efficiently and with ease, the job lacks challenge and they should move up. However, as Peter says, 'The problem is that when you find something you can't do very well, that is where you stay, bungling your job, frustrating your co-workers, and eroding the effectiveness of the organization.'

The Peter Principle has only been accepted as common parlance because it reflects a fundamental problem when assessing potential. We know, or we think we know, that someone is good at his or her present job. But does this predict success in the next one up? Perhaps yes, perhaps no; however, we cannot be sure because the skills needed by, for example, a first-rate research scientist are quite different from those required by the leader of a research team. Technical competence does not necessarily indicate managerial competence.

Beating the Peter Principle – for yourself

Can the Peter Principle be beaten? The answer is yes, but with difficulty. People don't usually refuse promotion. If they do, they become suspect. It is thought that they should be made of sterner stuff. It is, however, perfectly reasonable to check on what is involved if you are promoted. You should obtain precise answers to questions on what you will be expected to achieve, the resources you will be given to achieve it and the problems you will meet. If you think these demands are unreasonable, discuss the job to see if they can be modified.

Don't take a job unless you are satisfied that you can do it, or at least that you can learn how to do it within an acceptable period of time. You can quite properly ask what training and help you will be given in the early stages. If your predecessor failed, you can ask what went wrong, so that you can avoid making the same mistakes.

Beating the Peter Principle – for others

If you are in a position of offering promotion or a new job, you have to be aware of the Peter Principle and how to circumvent it. You need to match the capacities of the candidate to the demands of the job, and your starting point for this process should be an in-depth analysis of the skills required. These should be classified under the headings of MATCH:

- *Managerial* – making things happen, leading, inspiring and motivating people, team building and maintaining morale, coordinating and directing effort, using resources productively, and controlling events to achieve the required results.

- *Analytical* – dissecting problems and coming up with the right conclusions about what is happening and what should happen.

- *Technical/professional* – an understanding not only of all the tricks of the trade but also of how to use other people's knowledge effectively.

- *Communications* – putting the message across.

- *Human resource management* – the ability to persuade, enthuse and motivate; trustworthiness, integrity, dedication.

When you have drawn up the specifications, measure the candidate against each of these criteria. Obtain whatever evidence you can about his or her performance in the present job that gives any indication of potential competence in these areas. Ask for information on successes and failures and why they occurred.

This matching process should identify any potential weaknesses. You can then discuss these and decide on any help the individual needs in the shape of coaching, training or further experience.

Monitor the progress of the individual carefully in the initial months. Your aim should be to spot dangerous tendencies in good time so that swift remedial action can be taken.

Military incompetence

Norman Dixon suggests that there are two basic types of military incompetents. The first group includes Generals Elphinstone (first Afghan war), Raglan (the Crimean War), Butler (Boer War) and Percival (Singapore). These were all mild, courteous and peaceful men, paralysed by the burden of decision-making under fire. The second group includes people like Haig, Joffre and a number of other First World War generals. They are characterized by overweening ambition coupled with a terrifying insensitivity to the suffering of others. Far from being paralysed by decisions, they were active, but active in vain, devious, scheming and dishonest ways. Alistair Mant,[3] in *Leaders We Deserve*, quotes the example of the catastrophic results achieved in the Crimean War when an incompetent in the first group (Raglan) has authority over someone in the second group (the Earl of Cardigan, reputed by one contemporary to possess the 'brains of a horse').

The elements of military incompetence are listed by Norman Dixon as:

- serious wastage of human resources;
- fundamental conservatism and clinging to outworn tradition or to past successes;
- tendency to reject or ignore information that is unpalatable or that conflicts with preconceptions (as with company 'yes men');
- tendency to underestimate the enemy;
- indecisiveness and a tendency to abdicate from the role of decision-maker;
- obstinate persistence in a given task despite strong contrary evidence;
- failure to exploit a situation gained and a tendency to 'pull punches';
- failure to make adequate reconnaissance;
- a predilection for frontal assaults, often against the enemy's strongest point (reference the gross overcrowding of once profitable markets);

- belief in brute force rather than the clever ruse;
- failure to make use of surprise or deception;
- undue readiness to find scapegoats;
- suppression or distortion of news from the Front, usually deemed necessary for morale or security;
- belief in mystical forces – fate, bad luck, etc.

Examples of all these can be found in the actions or inactions of business leaders and managers:

- *Wasting resources* – most businesses are overstaffed, to the tune of 10 per cent or more.

- *Conservatism* – 'That's the way it has always worked. We have been market leaders for the last 20 years, why change?'

- *Rejecting unpalatable information* – 'What did you say about our losing market share? I don't believe it; these desk surveys are always inaccurate.'

- *Underestimating the enemy* – 'What's this? Bloggs & Co have introduced a new product in our range. And you think it will compete? Forget it. They're useless. They couldn't run a winkle stall.'

- *Indecisiveness* – 'We need to think a bit more about this.' 'I need more information.' 'I sometimes think that if you put problems like this in the "too difficult" section of your pending tray, they will go away.' 'It seems to me that we have several alternative routes ahead of us. Let's call a meeting next week or sometime to look at the pros and cons.' 'This is something for the board.'

- *Obstinate persistence* – 'Don't confuse me with the facts.' 'That's the way it's going to be.'

- *Failure to exploit a situation* – 'OK, you think we're going to exceed budget on our launch and you want to accelerate the programme. But let's not get too excited, we mustn't overstretch ourselves.'

- *Failure to reconnoitre* – 'I don't believe in market research.'

- *A predilection for frontal assaults* – 'Bloggs are doing particularly well in widgets. Yes, I appreciate we know nothing about widgets, but we can soon find out. Let's get in there fast and topple them from their perch.'

- *A belief in brute force* – 'Tell the union they can either take 5 per cent or do the other thing... What's this about a productivity package? I don't believe in messing about. It's a straight offer or nothing... They'll come out? I don't believe it.'

- *A failure to make use of surprise* – 'I don't like playing about. Let's get this show on the road... You think we'll get off to a better start if we keep the competition guessing? Forget it, we're miles better than they are!'

- *Scapegoating* – 'It's not us, it's the rate of exchange.' 'This xxxx government has screwed us up!' 'Why am I surrounded by incompetent fools?'

- *Suppression of news* – 'Don't tell them about how well we're doing. They'll only ask for more money.'

- *A belief in mystical forces* – 'I just feel in my bones we must do this thing.'

Why things go wrong – a summary

The main reasons for things going wrong are:

- inability to learn from mistakes;
- sheer incompetence through over-promotion;
- poor selection and inadequate training;
- overconfidence;
- underconfidence;
- carelessness;
- laziness;
- lack of foresight.

What can you do about it?

You may be forced to carry out a troubleshooting exercise as described in Chapter 47, but there are other things you can remember and do as set out below.

Inability to learn from mistakes

Remember Murphy's Law, which states that if anything can go wrong it will. Mistakes will happen. The unforgivable thing is to make the same mistake twice. You learn from your mistakes by analysing what went wrong – no excuses, no alibis – and making notes of what to do and what not to do next time.

Incompetence

This is something you should minimize in your subordinates by a constant drive to improve selection and performance standards and by training and coaching aimed at correcting specified weaknesses.

If you have doubts about your own ability, analyse your own strengths and weaknesses and grab every opportunity you can to get extra training and advice from people you believe in. If that still does not work, get out in good time.

Poor selection, inadequate training

If you pick the wrong person for the job they will underperform and make mistakes. You must ensure that you specify exactly what you want in terms of experience, qualifications, knowledge, skills and personality, and that you do not settle for second best. Your interview should be planned systematically to find out what the candidate has to offer under each of the headings of your specification. Ensure by probing questions that you establish whether or not the experience is of the right sort and at the right level. Ask for details of achievements. Check that the candidate has had a progressive career with no record of failures or mysterious gaps. Check by telephone with the present or previous employer that the candidate has told you the truth about his job, period of employment and, where appropriate, reason for leaving.

If you have failed to provide proper induction training, or to take the right steps to identify and meet individuals' training needs, you should not be surprised if they are not up to the job. Guidance on approaches to developing people is given in Chapter 9.

Overconfidence

This is the most difficult problem to eradicate. It is always said in the Royal Air Force that the most accident-prone pilots are the over-confident ones. You need confidence in yourself and your staff. How can it be controlled from going over the edge?

It takes time to understand or demonstrate that misjudgements occur because you are so certain that you know all the answers that no attempt is made to foresee or take care of the unexpected. Over-confident people tend to have tunnel vision – they can see quite clearly to the end but they take no notice of what is happening on either side or beyond. And if they see the light at the end of the tunnel they may not appreciate that it is the light of an oncoming train.

Underconfidence

This can be overcome as long as the individual is fundamentally competent. People who lack confidence often need help from someone who can underline achievements and provide encouragement to do more of the same. Mentors can help, as can a deliberate policy of extending people steadily so that they are not suddenly faced with a daunting leap in the level of work they have to do. Start by giving underconfident people tasks that are well within their capabilities and progressively increase demands, but only in achievable steps.

Carelessness

This is a universal problem. It can happen through overconfidence, but we all make mistakes under pressure or because we think the task is easier than it is. Sadly, reputations can be damaged, even destroyed by relatively minor mistakes. If you submit a report to your board with a glaring arithmetical error in it, the credibility of your whole report may be damaged, even if the mistake, although obvious, was not significant. Never submit a report or write a key letter without checking every figure and every fact at least once. If possible, ask someone else to do it as well.

Laziness

No one would ever admit to being lazy. But lazy people do exist, either because they are naturally indolent or because they have not been given sufficient leadership and a well-defined role in the organization. If one of your staff is lazy, put the boot in. It cannot be tolerated.

Lack of foresight

This is a common reason for errors. As a manager, one of your prime responsibilities is to think ahead. You must try to anticipate all the eventualities and make contingency plans accordingly. You won't get it right every time and you may find yourself occasionally in a crisis-management situation. But you will at least be better prepared if thought has been given to some of the eventualities, even if you could not anticipate them all.

Endnotes

1 Peter, L J (1972) *The Peter Principle*, Allen & Unwin, London

2 Dixon, N F (1979) *On the Psychology of Military Incompetence*, Futura, London

3 Mant, A (1985) *Leaders We Deserve*, Blackwell, London

PART FIVE
Business and financial management

How to be businesslike

A businesslike approach to management focuses on allocating resources to business opportunities and making the best use of them to achieve the required results. Managers who are businesslike understand and act upon:

- the business imperatives of the organization – its mission and its strategic goals;

- the organization's business model – the basis upon which its business is done (how its mission and strategic goals will be achieved);

- the organization's business drivers – the characteristics of the business that move it forward;

- the organization's core competencies – what the business is good at doing;

- the factors that will ensure the effectiveness of its activities including specific issues concerning profitability, productivity, financial budgeting and control, costs and benefits, customer service and operational performance;

- the key performance indicators (KPIs) of the business (the results or outcomes identified as being crucial to the achievement of high performance) that can be used to measure progress towards attaining goals;

- the factors that will ensure that the firm's resources, especially its human resources, create sustained competitive advantage because they are valuable, imperfectly imitable and non-substitutable.

How to make a business case   51

A business case sets out the reasons why a proposed course of action will benefit the business, how it will provide that benefit and how much it will cost. The case should be made either in added value terms (ie the income generated by the proposal will significantly exceed the cost of implementing it), or on the basis of the return on investment (ie the cost of the investment, say in training, is justified by the financial returns in such areas as increased productivity).

The basis for a business case

Clearly, a business case is more convincing when it is accompanied by realistic projections of the return on investment. The case for capital expenditure can be made by an analysis of the cash flows associated with the investment and appraisals of the benefits that are likely to arise from them. The object is to demonstrate that in return for paying out a given amount of cash today, a larger amount will be received over a period of time. There are a number of investment appraisal techniques available such as payback, the accounting rate of return, discounted cash flow and net present value. The case for a new product idea can be based on answers to the following questions:

- Does it meet a well-defined consumer need?
- In what segment of the market can this product be sold?
- In what way does this product provide more value to customers than existing products with which it would compete?

- Can it be differentiated adequately from alternative products?
- How well does it fit in with the existing product range?
- Does it exploit the company's existing skills and resources?
- What investment is required in developing and marketing the new product?
- What is the likely return on that investment?

Making the business case can be more difficult in areas where it is hard to generate convincing estimates of future income, for example, when justifying investment in training. But an attempt should be made. In this example, training investment was justified because it would:

- improve individual, team and corporate performance in terms of output, quality, speed and overall productivity;
- attract high-quality employees by offering them learning and development opportunities, increasing their levels of competence and enhancing their skills, thus enabling them to obtain more job satisfaction, to gain higher rewards and to progress within the organization;
- improve operational flexibility by extending the range of skills possessed by employees (multiskilling);
- increase the commitment of employees by encouraging them to identify with the mission and objectives of the organization;
- help to manage change by increasing understanding of the reasons for change and providing people with the knowledge and skills they need to adjust to new situations;
- provide line managers with the skills required to manage and develop their people;
- help to develop a positive culture in the organization – one, for example, which is orientated towards performance improvement;
- provide higher levels of service to customers;
- minimize learning costs (reduce the length of learning curves).

Enhancing the business case

A business case will be enhanced if:

- It can be shown convincingly that the return on investment meets or exceeds the amount required by company policy and that the immediate costs are not going have detrimental effects on cash flow.

- Data are made available on the impact the proposal is likely to make on key areas of the organization's operations, such as customer service levels, quality, shareholder value, productivity, income generation, innovation, skills development and talent management.

- It can be shown that the proposal will increase the business's competitive edge, for example ensuring that it can achieve competitive advantage through innovation and/or reducing time-to-market.

- There is proof that the innovation has already worked well within the organization (perhaps as a pilot scheme) or represents 'good practice' that is likely to be transferable to the organization.

- It can be implemented without too much trouble, for example not taking up a lot of managers' time.

- It will add to the reputation of the company by showing that it is a 'world class' organization: that what it does is as good as, if not better than, the world leaders in the sector in which the business operates (a promise that publicity will be achieved through articles in professional journals, press releases and conference presentations will help).

- The proposal is brief, to the point and well argued – it should take no more than five minutes to present orally and should be summarized in writing on the proverbial one side of one sheet of paper (supplementary details can be included in appendices).

Making the case

As a manager, you may have to make out your case in a presentation to follow up a written business case or on its own. You have to persuade people to believe in your views and accept your recommendations. To do this, you must have a clear idea of what you want, and you have to show that you believe in it yourself. Above all, the effectiveness of your presentation will depend upon the care with which you have prepared it.

Preparation

Thorough preparation is vital. You must think through not only what should be done and why, but also how people will react. Only then can you decide how to make your case, stressing the benefits without underestimating the costs, and anticipating objections.

You should think of the questions your audience is likely to raise, and answer them in advance, or at least have your answers ready. The most likely questions are:

What:

- is the proposal?
- will be the benefit?
- will it cost?
- are the facts, figures, forecasts and assumptions upon which the proposal is based?
- are the alternatives?

Why:

- should we change what we are doing now?
- is this proposal or solution better than the alternatives?

How:

- is the change to be made?

- are the snags to be overcome?
- have the alternatives been examined?
- am I affected by the change?

Who:

- will be affected by the change and what will be their reaction?
- is likely to have the strongest views for or against the change, and why?
- will implement the proposal?

When:

- should this be done?

To make your case you have to do three things:

1 Show that it is based on a thorough analysis of the facts and that the alternatives were properly evaluated before the conclusion was reached. If you have made assumptions, you must demonstrate that these are reasonable on the basis of relevant experience and justifiable projections that allow for the unexpected. Bear in mind Robert Heller's words[1] that 'a proposal is only as strong as its weakest assumption'.

2 Spell out the benefits – to the company and the individuals to whom the case is being made. Present your case 'sunny side up'. Wherever possible, express benefits in financial terms. Abstract benefits, such as customer satisfaction or workers' morale, are difficult to sell. But don't produce 'funny numbers' – financial justification that will not stand up to examination.

3 Reveal costs. Don't try to disguise them in any way. And be realistic. Your proposition will be destroyed if anyone can show that you have underestimated the costs.

Remember, boards want to know in precise terms what they will get for their money. Most boards are cautious, being unwilling and often unable to take much risk. For this reason, it is difficult to make a case for experiments or pilot schemes unless the board, committee or individual can see what the benefits and the ultimate bill will be.

Case presentation

Your proposal will often be made in two stages: a written report followed by an oral presentation. The quality of the latter will often tip the balance in your favour (or against you). Effective speaking and writing reports are dealt with in Chapters 42 and 43 respectively, but it is appropriate to note at this stage some special points you should bear in mind when making a case orally in front of an audience:

1 Your presentation should not just consist of a repetition of the facts in a written case. It should be used to put across the main points of the argument, leaving out the detail.

2 Do not assume that your audience has read the written report or understood it. While you are talking, try to avoid referring to the report. This may switch people's attention from what you are saying. Use visual aids, preferably a flip chart, to emphasize the main points. But don't overdo this – it is possible to be too slick. The audience will be convinced by you, not by your elegant visual aids.

3 Make sure your opening secures people's attention. They must be immediately interested in your presentation. Begin by outlining your plan, its benefits and its costs, and let the audience know how you are going to develop your case.

4 Bring out the disadvantages and the alternative courses of action so that you are not suspected of concealing or missing something.

5 Avoid being drawn into too much detail. Be succinct and to the point.

6 An emphatic summing up is imperative. It should convey with complete clarity what you want the board, committee or individual to do.

The effectiveness of your presentation will be largely dependent on how well you have prepared – not only putting your facts, figures and arguments clearly down on paper but also deciding what you are going to say at the meeting and how you are going to say it. The more important the case, the more carefully you should rehearse the presentation.

Checklist

- Do you know exactly what you want?
- Do you really believe in your case?
- Have you obtained and checked all the facts that support your case?
- What are the strongest arguments for your case?
- Why must the present situation be changed?
- Who else will be affected? Unions, other divisions or departments?
- What are the arguments against your plan?
- What alternatives are there to your plan?
- To whom are you presenting your plan? Have you done any lobbying?
- Have you discussed the finances with the experts?
- Do you know who are your probable allies and who are likely to be your opponents?
- Have you prepared handouts of any complicated figures?
- Have you discussed the best time to present your case?
- Your ideas were good when you first thought of them, but are they still as good?

Endnote

1 Heller, R (1982) *The Business of Success*, Sidgwick & Jackson, London

How to prepare 52
a business plan

What is a business plan?

A business plan sets out what you or your business intend to achieve and how you intend to achieve it in order to attract any investment required. The plan includes financial projections of revenue and profit based on business forecasts covering the planned levels of sales or activity, the income they will generate and the investment required to get the expected results. In addition, it will provide information in sufficient but not excessive detail on how those results will be achieved.

Why have a plan?

A business plan may be required for any of the following reasons:

- to convince some person or organization, such as a bank, a finance company or a senior executive in the company, to invest in your business or idea;
- to convince someone to join with you in the business;
- to help in selling a business;
- to obtain a grant or regulatory approval.

Importantly, the discipline of producing a business plan and then using it as a point of reference can also provide a basis for driving and managing a business.

How should a business plan be structured?

The structure of a business plan will vary according to its purpose and the type of business it is dealing with. The following are typical headings, based on those suggested by Brian Finch in *How to Write a Business Plan* (Kogan Page):[1]

- summary;
- the business background;
- the proposal;
- financial projections;
- supporting information on the market, operations, finance, control systems, management and personnel;
- a risk assessment;
- conclusion.

Summary

This should be short (no more than one page long) and give anyone who may not be inclined to read a lengthy document the essential information they need to attract their attention. The key points to be made include a brief description of the business, the essence of the plan (what you intend to do), why you believe the plan will succeed, the investment of cash required and the return expected from that investment.

The business background

Describe the essence of the business – what is produced or what services are provided, its markets, customers and suppliers, and an outline of its trading history unless it is a start-up business.

The proposal

The proposal is the heart of the business plan. It sets out:

- *What you intend to do* – this is an explicit statement describing what you expect to achieve in quantified terms and how the scale of your achievement will be measured.

- *When you are going to do it* – the period of time covered by the plan. This should be realistic. A plan extending for more than five years is taking you too far ahead to be believable. Three years or so is often a more acceptable timetable.

- *How you intend to do it* – this is a description of your plan of action, specifying the sequence of steps you will take.

- *Why you believe you will be successful* – this is an important part of the proposal. The aim is to make a convincing case for your plan based on what you will be offering to customers, their likely response, an analysis of the competition and a description of the resources you will be able to marshal when implementing the plan. This case is reinforced by the later sections of the plan covering finance, the market, operations, management and personnel, control systems and risk assessment.

- *What you need to finance the plan* – this spells out how much cash you will need and when you will need it. If applicable, an indication is made of the amount of cash that you can already make available and, therefore, how much more you will need from an investor or investors. This should be a realistic sum – not too much and not too little.

- *The financial returns your plan will generate* – this is a summary statement of the returns an investor can anticipate from an investment, which is expanded in the section on financial projections.

Financial projections

Financial forecasts are required over the period of the plan, say three years. They should state for each product or service group the anticipated sales and the gross profit or margin (the difference between sales revenue and the cost of goods sold) year by year. It is also helpful to include under the same headings a summary of trading results, if applicable, over the past two or three years.

These projections should not go into elaborate detail. They can be expanded in an appendix.

It is necessary to explain the basis for the projections – why you think the sales and gross profit figures will be achieved. Refer as necessary to other sections in the plan where this is covered in more detail, for example a marketing plan. Figures that have been affected by such things as a change in the product mix, the injection of extra resources into marketing or streamlining production or distribution, or reductions anticipated in unit costs should also be explained.

The market

Describe:

- who your existing customers are and who your new customers will be;
- why they buy an existing product or service or will be keen to buy a new product or service, emphasizing any particular features that will persuade existing customers to buy more or will attract new ones;
- the current size of the market;
- trends in the size of the market – ideally it should be growing, but if it is static or declining you have to show convincingly that you can buck the trend and increase your market share or obtain a reasonable amount of market share on entry;
- the location(s) of the market – local, national or international;
- the competitors – who they are or might be, the existing and potential strength of the competition as measured by market share;
- why you believe you can achieve sustained competitive advantage and beat the competition with your product or service in terms of quality, cost, level of customer service, the uniqueness of your product or service, or the special characteristics of your operation in terms of the people you employ, the technology you use, your research and development expertise and the effectiveness of your distribution system;

- your pricing strategy;
- your marketing plans – sales, promotion, advertising and distribution.

Operations

Summarize the main processes used in your business so that investors can be confident that these will support the achievement of your business goals. Examples of processes include research and development, manufacturing, distribution, retailing, wholesaling, customer service, service operations, use of the internet, advertising and promotions. Indicate the extent to which your market assessments and sales projections have been based on rigorous market research and market testing.

Management and personnel

Give brief details of the qualifications, experience and achievement of yourself and the rest of the management team and why you have the collective expertise to achieve the plan. Also summarize the skills of your key workers and why they will contribute to the success of the enterprise.

Control systems

Outline the systems in place for managing and controlling the business in order to convince readers of the plan that you have the capability to run the operation effectively and efficiently. The systems could include accounting (budgeting and control), production control, service level control, quality control, sales analysis and control, and analysis of customer service levels.

Risk assessment

It is advisable to demonstrate in the plan that you are aware of any risks involved (no one believes that implementing business plans does not involve some risk) and how you intend to manage those risks. This shows that you have considered the plan from all the angles.

Conclusion

A brief conclusion is necessary that simply includes words to the effect that you commend the plan as being realistic, achievable and a basis for generating an acceptable return for anyone who invests in the business.

How should the plan be presented?

The plan needs to make a good impression and then hold the attention of the reader. To do this it must be clearly laid out with headings and sub-headings to provide signposts to take people through the text. Short sharp sentences should be used with action words saying what you will do and when. Avoid jargon.

The plan should be evidence based. Proposals should be supported by reliable and verifiable facts and figures wherever possible. As Brian Finch says in Kogan Page's *How to Write a Business Plan*:[1]

> Whatever you do don't waffle! It is common to read reports that go on at great length about the market, the opportunity, the history of the project and so on, but without any evidence. The plan may be badly or beautifully written but the attention of the business partner or divisional chief executive or financier will be lost at the beginning when they get bored and decide they don't believe the hype.

Endnote

1 Finch, B (2016) *How to Write a Business Plan*, Kogan Page, London

How to budget   53

The need for budgets

Budgets don't win friends but they do influence people. They can be painful to create and can be agonizing to manage. But they do translate policy into financial terms and, whether we like it or not, that is the way in which plans must be expressed and, ultimately, performance controlled.

Budgets are needed for three reasons:

1 to show the financial implications of plans;
2 to define the resources required to achieve the plans;
3 to provide a means of measuring, monitoring and controlling results against the plans.

The process of budgeting

The process of budgeting consists of the following steps:

1 Budget guidelines are prepared that are derived from the corporate plan and forecasts. They will include sales and outputs targets, the activity levels for which the budget has to cater, and assumptions on inflation, costs and prices. Policies will be set on the profit margins or financial contribution to be achieved. Targets for reducing the budget may be set.

2 Initial budgets setting out proposed expenditure under each heading are prepared by the budget holder. Changes to previous budgets that are not in line with changes in activity levels or inflation, costs and price assumptions have to be justified. Naturally, a budget that failed to achieve the targeted reduction would have to be explained.

3 Draft budgets are checked first by budget accountants and then by higher management to ensure that they meet the guidelines and any increases in expenditure are justified.

4 Subject to any amendment, which may arise from iterative discussion, approved budgets are issued to budget holders as a control document.

5 Control is exercised over expenditure by comparing actuals with the budgeted figure. If there is a difference – a 'variance' – this will have to be justified.

Limitations of budgets

The main problems of budgets are:

- The basic budgeting procedure is inadequate: imprecise guidelines, unsatisfactory background data, cumbersome systems, lack of technical advice and assistance to managers, arbitrary cuts by top management.

- There is an unskilled or cynical approach by managers to budgeting resulting from inadequate basic procedures, lack of guidance, training or encouragement, or a feeling that budgets are simply weapons to be deployed against them rather than tools for them to use.

- There is a lack of accurate forecasts of future activity levels.

- Unrealistic assumptions are made as a basis for budgeting.

- Targets for reducing costs are unrealistic and unachievable.

- It is difficult to amend the budget in response to changing circumstances.

- The fundamental weakness of basing budgets on past levels of expenditure that are simply 'plussed up' rather than subjecting the whole budget to a critical examination.

- There are weaknesses in reporting or controlling procedures that prevent the budget being used to monitor performance.

Preparing budgets

The problems concerning the preparation of budgets mentioned above can be eliminated or at least reduced if the following actions are taken:

1 Prepare budget guidelines that set out policies on where you want to go and, broadly, how you intend to get there. These could be set as targets for activity levels such as sales or output, or as an outline of major operating plans. Base any assumptions to be used in budgeting, such as rates of inflation and predicted increases in costs or prices, on properly researched information.

2 Set realistic targets for cost reductions. If a corporate cost reduction exercise is laying down the cuts required, at least explain why it is necessary. Help and guidance might be required on the priorities to be attached to different activities and therefore the scope for cutting costs.

3 Ensure that those responsible for preparing budgets are given advice and encouragement by management or budget accountants. These experts should be there to help, not to prod or threaten, as they have been known to do.

4 Train budget holders in the budgeting process, especially newly appointed managers. It will be a technique with which many people are unfamiliar and they will need all the help they can get.

5 Get people to think hard about their budgets. They should be discouraged from simply updating last year's actual expenditures. Wherever there is any choice on how much is spent, they should be asked to go back to first principles and justify the expenditure. For major items, they could be required to make out a proper business case that sets out the returns expected on the expenditure. Budget estimates should be based on reliable forecasts of future activity levels and costs, which should be included in supporting documentation. As far as possible, each existing and proposed activity should be analysed to establish: its objectives, what is involved, why it is being carried out or is to be carried out, the present and projected costs of the activity, the benefits resulting from the activity and the key performance indicators that can be used to assess the success of the activity.

6 Do not accept any large increase on last year's budget without an explanation and a justification.

7 Be wary of even a large decrease. This could mean that a significant activity is being marginalized to be replaced by one that is not going to be so productive.

8 Probe to ensure that budgets submitted to you are realistic and do not include a 'fudge' factor – sums of money that will be put on one side to cover overspends.

9 Do not slash budgets arbitrarily. Give reasons. If you don't, you will get fudge factors or a 'couldn't care less' attitude.

10 Update or 'flex' budgets regularly, especially when activity levels and costs are subject to large variations.

Flexible budgets

If it is possible, with a reasonable degree of accuracy, to relate changes in income and costs to levels of activity, the use of flexible budgets is worthwhile. Budgets are 'flexed' when the original budget is deliberately amended to take account of changed activity levels. A static budget is prepared for only one level of activity, such as the volume of sales. This means that both fixed and variable costs are assumed to remain constant at any level of activity. Fixed costs may do so, but variable costs by definition will not. Because the actual activity or output is almost certainly different from the budgeted activity, the original budget will be inaccurate and a false picture will be presented of variances from that budget. It is therefore necessary to flex the budget to reflect different levels of activity. This is done by assuming different levels of activity and preparing cost and overhead budgets for each level.

The control of a flexible budget is carried out on the same basis as any other control process; that is to say, actuals are compared with budget to show any variance. However, the budget with which the actuals are compared is the adjusted budget based on actual activity levels.

Budgetary control

Expenditures against budget have to be monitored by the budget holder so that variances can be dealt with in good time. Budget actuals will be scrutinized by budget or management account-ants and variance reports prepared for budget holders and higher management. Budget holders are held to account for any variances and will be expected to take corrective action.

This sounds simple but isn't. A successful budgetary control procedure is not easy to achieve. You have to work at it. There is no problem in designing a system with computer-generated reports containing lots of information. But there is a danger of generating information overload with excessively complex data. The answer is to keep it simple so that variances stare budget holders and their managers in the face and provide a driving force for action.

How to cut costs

Costs always need controlling. You should start with the assumption that costs are too high and can be reduced. This assumption is based on the knowledge that many companies have not only survived but also flourished after drastic cost-cutting exercises. When you remove the fat that always exists you are left with a leaner and more powerful organization.

What to cut

Your attack on costs should concentrate on these six areas:

- *Employee costs* – in labour-intensive companies, employee costs may exceed 50 per cent of income. Over-employment, especially in service and staff departments, is a major contributory cause of excessive costs. Employment costs will include the direct costs of salaries, wages, pensions (a considerable item) and other benefits, and the indirect cost of the HR and training functions.

- *Manufacturing costs* – these are the actual costs incurred in making products; they reflect labour, material and operating costs, but also, importantly, the way the product has been designed.

- *Selling costs* – these may be largely accounted for by the cost of employees in the sales, customer service or distribution functions, although this will be covered under employee costs. The figures will also include advertising, promotions, public relations, packaging and display material.

- *Development costs* – these are the costs of developing new products, processes, materials and systems, especially IT, and of acquiring new businesses.

- *Material and inventory costs* – the cost of buying materials and bought-in parts and of maintaining optimum stock levels. The latter can be particularly high if inventory control systems are ineffective.

- *Operating costs* – all the other costs incurred in running the business. These include space, facilities, IT, the provision of plant and equipment and all the services required to keep the organization going.

Waste and costly activities

Any examination-of-costs exercise should first focus on wasteful practices and costly activities. The areas where they can occur should be identified before conducting a cost-cutting exercise so that attention can be directed to likely trouble spots. Concentrate on both practices or procedures that can lead to waste or pointless costs, and on areas where employees can waste time or incur unnecessary expenditure.

Waste can occur in any of the following areas:

- over-complex procedures with unnecessary forms and reports;
- too much unnecessary traffic on the intranet;
- focusing so much on achieving output or service standards that attention is diverted from the cost of doing so;
- too much checking and verifying of work;
- too many indecisive meetings;
- too many layers of management and supervision;
- delays in decision-making because authority is not delegated down the line;
- over-rigid adherence to rules and regulations;
- bottlenecks and inefficient work flows.

Time-wasting practices by staff can include lateness or leaving early, prolonged tea or meal breaks, unnecessary breaks for any other reason, spending time on the internet and dealing with personal matters in company time. Other wasteful practices include extravagant use of the company's facilities.

Cost-creating practices can include absenteeism and frequent absences through illness. A major cost for all retail companies and other businesses too is pilfering.

Planning to cut costs

First you build cost-effectiveness into your plans. Then you introduce or improve procedures such as budgeting that define and justify the costs that it is reasonable to incur. You later control expenditure against the budget, probing into over-expenditure, finding out why it is happening and initiating corrective action.

Plans should be based on cost–benefit studies that aim to find the best ratio between expenditure and results; in other words, to minimize costs and maximize benefits. The emphasis should be on realism. It is good to be forward looking and entrepreneurial. But if you are like that, you are always in danger of becoming euphoric about the future, overestimating the benefits and underestimating the costs. At the planning stage, you must think hard about the costs you are likely to incur. You must be realistic. It will almost certainly cost more than you think (or than your suppliers tell you it will cost). Find out what you are really going to spend by analysis and obtaining estimates from a number of people. Add at least 10 per cent for contingencies. Insist on penalty clauses to recover costs in the event of an overspend. Query every request for a change in a specification or for something extra, and insist on a cost estimate. Allow for inflation and fluctuation in exchange rates. Always expect the worse.

You should be equally realistic about benefits. Business cases are littered with overestimates of benefits as well as underestimates of costs. Challenge every assumption. Carry out a 'sensitivity analysis' to determine the effects on income and costs of optimistic, realistic and pessimistic forecasts of performance.

The cost-reduction exercise

A cost-reduction exercise is a planned campaign aimed at cutting costs by a specified amount. It requires three initial steps, the careful allocation of responsibility for the exercise and the application of a searching, deliberate, carefully controlled and consistent approach to conducting it.

Initial steps

Set targets, either for immediate cuts in crisis conditions or for specific reductions in the short term (defined in weeks rather than months). Targets may call for an overall reduction of costs by, say, 10 per cent or for cutting overheads by a certain percentage. Or they may be set in specific areas, eg a 10 per cent reduction in staffing. They can be expressed in the form of ratio improvement, for example reducing the ratio of labour costs to sales from 11 to 10 per cent.

The significant impact of overheads on profits should be emphasized to everyone. It is interesting to note that in a company where profits are 10 per cent of sales, a reduction in the ratio of labour costs to sales from 11 to 10 per cent would increase profits by 10 per cent. It all ends up on the bottom line and that is what counts.

Productivity targets expressed in financial terms, such as 'reduce costs per unit of output by 3 per cent', may be less immediate but they can usefully be incorporated in a set of cost-reduction targets as longer-term objectives. Increases in productivity can be obtained by reducing costs in relation to output, or by increasing output in relation to costs or, preferably, by both reducing costs and increasing output. The message must be got across that unit costs are there to be attacked at all times – after all, they aggregate into total costs. Get down to basics: the shop floor, the distribution centre, the retail unit or the general office. This is where the main costs are incurred. Keep it simple. Look at specific items. Don't accept excuses. Compare and contrast to identify areas where costs are excessive. Benchmark similar organizations to find out what their cost ratios are and what they are doing about optimizing them. You can learn a lot from the experiences of other people. Competitors are not going to cooperate, but comparable organizations that are broadly similar to yours in different manufacturing or retailing areas may do so. Employers' and trade associations can help with information.

Decide where to cut – typically, the most fruitful areas are in employment costs (reducing headcounts) and wasteful practices. It is remarkable how often departmental managers who scream with pain when they are told to cut their staff by, say, 10 per cent will cope quite well afterwards. People responsible for cost-reduction exercises will claim and prove that they can always cut staff numbers by 15 per cent or even more without reducing efficiency.

Decide how to cut – allocating responsibilities, drawing up the programme and implementing it.

Responsibility for the cost-reduction exercise

The most important thing to do is to appoint as senior an executive as possible, preferably a full-time member of the board, to direct the cost-reduction exercise. He or she should have drive, energy, determination and, most important, the authority and courage to implement measures, however unpleasant some of them may be.

The question of who is to assist this executive then arises. You may consider using management consultants to help and advise on specific problem areas. But do not ask consultants to carry out the main task. If your organization is not capable of taking action itself, however drastic, it does not deserve to survive. In any case, consultants are expensive and this is supposed to be a cost-cutting exercise.

Neither should you set up a committee to control the exercise. Committees are obstacles to action. You might establish a small (not more than three people) project team of senior executives, but do not let them function as a standing committee with agendas, minutes and so on. Better still, give complete authority to one director to control the exercise to use whom he or she wants when he or she wants and to call meetings as she or he thinks fit.

The director in charge of the exercise needs terms of reference by which to operate. They should take the form of a set of targets to be achieved by a certain date or sequence of dates. If there are any constraints (eg don't sack the chairman's son-in-law) they should be mentioned now. The director should then be told the extent of his or her authority to make decisions and when and in what circumstances to report back. She or he can then proceed to carry out an initial survey of the situation and scope for cuts, and then solicit opinions about what needs to be done, gather the facts to support or refute those opinions, define the problem areas, decide what to do and draw up a programme for doing it.

Approach to the exercise

Successful cost-reduction exercises use the most simple of questioning techniques:

- What is done?
- Why is it done?
- Does it need to be done at all?
- If it needs to be done, can it be simplified or carried out more cheaply?

The following principles can be applied:

- Top managers must accept a revision of the administrator's task. Top management may have imposed or supported countless rules and regulations to ensure that the systems and methods used in the business are foolproof. These may seem to have been written on the assumption that all employees fall into two categories: stupid or crooked. It has been said that if you cast the administrator in the role of bureaucrat he will do it superbly. The paraphernalia of administrative systems and routines drawn up under this type of regime can only be swept away by top management.

- The price of perfection is prohibitive: sensible approximation costs less. In Voltaire's words: 'The best is the enemy of the good.'

Aim high but don't overstretch yourself in doing it. Productivity in administration means one person trying to reach 95 per cent efficiency and reaching it, rather than two people trying to reach 100 per cent and only reaching 90 per cent.

- Most employees can be trusted. If this principle is accepted, a wide range of checks and monitoring can be replaced by managers managing and team leaders leading. Thorough spot checks can be used to supplement day-to-day management and eliminate expensive and oppressive supervision.

- All staff can help to bring about the desired changes. Most people, if encouraged, will bring forward ideas to simplify and rationalize their work. Improvement groups can be formed to look at specific issues.

- Consider ways of cutting employment costs without compulsory redundancy. Discussions with employees and their union representatives can produce alternative ways such as part-time working for a temporary period.

- Staff can become too specialized. Too many specialists can produce unnecessary work and hinder flexibility. Specialists exist to serve and ease the running of the business, not to stifle initiative, become barriers to action or create yet another paper chain.

- Never legislate for every eventuality. Leave as much as possible to the common sense of those who are trusted in managerial positions.

- There is no substitute for personal probing into what is happening. You will find out more if you find out for yourself. Don't be afraid to conduct a sample first-hand investigation. A focused study can be more valuable than an all-embracing but superficial investigation.

How to read a   55
balance sheet

A balance sheet is a statement, on the last day of the accounting period, of the company's assets and liabilities and the share capital or the shareholders' investment in the company.

Balance sheet analysis assesses the financial strengths and weaknesses of the company, primarily from the point of view of the shareholders and potential investors. But as a manager you contribute to the overall task of management to exercise proper stewardship over the funds invested in the company and the assets in its care. You therefore need to know how to analyse a balance sheet.

Balance sheet analysis

With the help of balance sheet ratios, the analysis focuses on the balance sheet equation, considers the make-up of the balance sheet in terms of assets and liabilities, and examines the liquidity position (how much cash or easily realizable assets are available) and capital structure.

The balance sheet equation

The balance sheet equation is: Capital + Liabilities = Assets. Capital plus liabilities shows where the money comes from, and assets indicate where the money is now.

Make-up of the balance sheet

The balance sheet contains four major sections:

- *Assets or capital in use*, which is divided into long-term or fixed assets (eg land, buildings and plant) and current or short-term assets, which include bank balances and cash, debtors, stocks of goods and materials and work-in-progress.

- *Current liabilities*, which are the amounts that will have to be paid within 12 months of the balance sheet date.

- *Net current assets or working capital*, which are current assets less current liabilities. Careful control of working capital lies at the heart of efficient business performance.

- *Sources of capital*, which comprise share capital, reserves including retained profits, and long-term loans.

Liquidity analysis

Liquidity analysis is concerned with the extent to which the business has an acceptable quantity of cash and easily realizable assets to meet its needs. The analysis may be based on the ratio of current assets (cash, working capital, etc) to current liabilities (the working capital ratio). Too low a ratio may mean that the liquid resources are insufficient to cover short-term payments. Too high a ratio might indicate that there is too much cash or working capital and that they are therefore being badly managed. The working capital ratio is susceptible to 'window dressing', which is the manipulation of the working capital position by accelerating or delaying transactions near the year end.

Liquidity analysis also uses the 'quick ratio' of current assets minus stocks to current liabilities. This concentrates on the more realizable of the current assets and therefore provides a stricter test of liquidity than the working capital ratio. It is therefore called 'the acid test'.

Capital structure analysis

Capital structure analysis examines the overall means by which a company finances its operations, which is partly by the funds of their ordinary shareholders (equity) and partly by loans from banks and other lenders (debt). The ratio of long-term debt to ordinary shareholders' funds indicates 'gearing'. A company is said to be highly geared when it has a high level of loan capital as distinct from equity capital.

How to use financial ratios

56

Ratio analysis studies and compares financial ratios which identify relationships between quantifiable aspects of a company's activities. The object is to reveal factors and trends affecting business performance so that action can be taken.

Types of ratios

There are many types of ratios and a detailed list is provided in the author's *A Handbook of Management Techniques*, Chapter 12 (Kogan Page, 2006). The following is a selection of the key ratios.

Return on capital employed

$$\frac{\text{Trading or operating profit}}{\text{Total assets (fixed and current assets} - \text{current liabilities)}}$$

Earnings per share

$$\frac{\text{Profit after interest, tax and ordinary dividends but before extraordinary items}}{\text{Number of ordinary shares issued by the company}}$$

Return on sales

$$\frac{\text{Trading or operating profit}}{\text{Total sales}} \times 100$$

Asset turnover rate

$$\frac{\text{Total sales}}{\text{Assets}}$$

Overhead costs

$$\frac{\text{Overheads}}{\text{Sales}} \times 100$$

Cost per unit of output

$$\frac{\text{Production costs}}{\text{Output in units}}$$

Departmental/functional costs

$$\frac{\text{Costs incurred by department or function}}{\text{Sales}}$$

Gearing

$$\frac{\text{Long term loans plus preference shares}}{\text{Ordinary shareholders' funds}}$$

Dividend cover

$$\frac{\text{Profits available for paying ordinary dividends}}{\text{Ordinary dividends}}$$

Debtor turnover

$$\frac{\text{Sales}}{\text{Debtors}}$$

Stock turnover rate

$$\frac{\text{Cost of sales}}{\text{Stock}}$$

Productivity – profit per employee

$$\frac{\text{Trading profit}}{\text{Number of employees}}$$

Productivity – sales per employee

$$\frac{\text{Sales}}{\text{Number of employees}}$$

Productivity – output per employee

$$\frac{\text{Units produced or processed}}{\text{Number of employees}}$$

Use of ratios

Ratios by themselves mean nothing. They must always be compared with:

● a norm or target;

● previous ratios in order to assess trends; and

● the ratios achieved in other comparable companies (benchmarking).

Caution has to be exercised in using ratios. The following limitations should be taken into account:

1 Ratios are calculated from financial statements which are affected by the financial bases and policies adopted on such matters as depreciation and the valuation of stocks.

2 Financial statements do not represent a complete picture of the business but merely a collection of facts which can be expressed in monetary terms. These may not refer to other factors that affect performance.

3 Overuse of ratios as controls could be dangerous as it could lead simply to the improvement of the ratio rather than dealing with the significant issues. For example, the return on capital employed can be improved by reducing assets, not by increasing profits.

4 A ratio is the comparison of two figures, a numerator and a denominator. When comparing ratios, it may be difficult to determine whether differences are due to changes in the numerator, the denominator, or both.

INDEX